OUR LORD'S PARABLES

OUR LORD'S PARABLES

R. C. McQuilkin

ZONDERVAN PUBLISHING HOUSE
OF THE ZONDERVAN CORPORATION
GRAND RAPIDS, MICHIGAN 49506

OUR LORD'S PARABLES
Revised edition of *Studying Our Lord's Parables*
Copyright © 1980 by The Zondervan Corporation

Copyright 1929 by Columbia Bible School, Columbia, South Carolina, with the title *Studying Our Lord's Parables for Yourself* and copyright 1933 by Columbia Bible School with the title *Studying Our Lord's Parables*.

Library of Congress Cataloging in Publication Data

McQuilkin, Robert Crawford, 1886-1952.
    Our Lord's parables.

    Edition of 1933 published under title: Studying Our Lord's Parables.
    1. Jesus Christ—Parables—Study. I. Title.
BT377.M3   1980   226'.806   79-25518
ISBN 0-310-41541-1

Scripture quotations are from the Holy Bible, New International Version, copyright © 1978 by the New York International Bible Society. Used by permission.

Printed in the United States of America

83   84   85   86   87   88 — 10   9   8   7   6   5   4   3

Contents

Foreword

Christ's unique method of teaching by stories was very powerful. It was also confusing to many of His hearers.

These stories, or parables, are no less powerful today—and no less confusing to many people. Prominent theologians and lay persons, deceived by the apparent simplicity of parables, have misunderstood Christ's meaning; and the church has been plagued by the many distortions resulting from such misunderstanding.

However, it need not be so. Christ used parables to teach profound truth to His disciples. They were not given for the purpose of confusing His followers.

Our Lord's Parables is a little classic that has gone through several editions—and translation into Spanish. This work has helped many Christians because it offers a way to understand what Jesus was teaching in His parables. It is not merely an exposition; there are many of these. Nor is it a bare statement of hermeneutical principles. The method for correctly understanding parables is explained and then used step by step in uncovering the meaning of seventeen parables. An application to our own Christian living is also provided.

The need for such study is as acute today as it was when R. C. McQuilkin first put these studies into print. Zondervan Publishing House is to be commended for making these lucid studies readily available once more.

As we study our Lord's parables and come to a clearer understanding of what He is teaching us there, may it be for the purpose He intended: the transformation of life.

J. Robertson McQuilkin
President
Columbia Bible College

7

Preface to the Revised Edition

We count it a privilege to offer once again Robert C. McQuilkin's study of seventeen of the parables of Jesus. This work carefully examines both the setting and the narrative of a parable in an attempt to discover the central message of Christ's words.

Our Lord's Parables has a rich printing history. In 1929 Columbia Bible School published a portion of this material as *Studying Our Lord's Parables for Yourself.* In 1933 Zondervan Publishing House issued a new edition in which lessons were added and the title shortened to read *Studying Our Lord's Parables.* This edition was reprinted several times and was also translated into the Spanish language. The present revised edition consists of all of the material found in the 1933 edition, along with a foreword by the author's son, J. Robertson McQuilkin.

The foundation of these studies is the Word of God, and as a result they are as relevant for today's student of Scripture as they were for earlier readers. It is with this conviction and in order to make this work as functional as possible for today's reader that in this edition we have used the New International Version of the Bible and made minor editorial changes.

We trust that this study of the words of Christ will continue to serve the Christian community for individual enrichment, group study, and supplemental reading in the classroom.

THE PUBLISHER

Introduction

The parables of our Lord are miracles of teaching, and His miracles were parables in action. The people of His day saw the miracles but missed the parable being taught. They heard the parables but did not give heed to the miracle being taught.

No study of the Scriptures is more interesting and fascinating than the study of the parables of our Lord. They have gripped the hearts of men in all ages. Many who have never opened a Bible know something of the story of the lost son, and those who have never heard of the word *parable* know what is meant by a good Samaritan, seed sown in good soil, tares among the wheat, and making use of your talents. These and many other expressions have entered our common speech because our Lord made them so real and vivid in parables.

Two verses in the Gospel of John help to show us why we may expect wonderful things from a study of the parables. The first is John 7:46: "No one ever spoke the way this man does." How true this is of the parables!

The biographer of Daniel Webster tells us that one of the major factors in leading that giant intellect to the acceptance of the Bible as a supernatural book was his reading of our Lord's parables. The great statesman concluded that no merely human teacher could produce such masterpieces.

The other verse is John 17:8: "I gave them the words you gave me." As we read the parables, let us remember that these, along with the other sayings of our Lord, were given to Him by the mighty God to give to us. What a thrill it is to realize that a parable is the very word of God.

A Sunday school teacher was telling her class about the parables of the Savior and gave them that well-known defini-

tion: "A parable is an earthly story with a heavenly meaning."
The next week she asked who could remember what a parable
was. One child eagerly raised her hand. "A parable," she said,
"is a heavenly story with no earthly meaning."

Now, what this little girl said expresses the idea that many
people have about parables. "I always thought they were just
pretty little stories," a young woman confessed after she had
studied the parables and discovered that they gave her the
very truths she needed for her Christian life.

But there is a difficulty of another kind in studying the
parables. We are prone to glean too many meanings from
them. Great scholars who have studied the parables often give
us entirely different interpretations of even the most familiar
ones. For this reason lay persons who read the Bible have
supposed that the parables are great puzzles and that ordinary
people cannot know what the intended lesson is.

These facts show the importance of studying the parables
for ourselves. The beauty and profit of these stories will come
home to us in a new way as we learn both how to study them
and how to apply the principles that should be used in interpreting them.

As we go on in our study, we will find many reasons why
our Lord's parables have so gripped the human heart and why
they have especially claimed the attention and careful study of
Christians. They are matchless gems of teaching. No study
will ever exhaust them. We can go back to the same parable
repeatedly and get a fresh message each time. The most up-
to-date principles of teaching are illustrated in these parables
of the One who is rightly called the Teacher. All other true
teachers, of any subject matter, should learn from Him.

The Lord's parables are simple and yet most profound. A
child can understand and be gripped by the story. Yet those
who know most of the Bible and who are students of life will
continue to find new riches and depth in the parables.

One other reason may be added here for studying the parables: they cover the whole range of human problems. Studying them will give us the view of the Lord Jesus Christ, which is God's own view, on life—that is, on the relations of men with God and with one another.

Grouping the Parables

Many different groupings of the parables have been made to help those who study them. Our Lord's teachings are so rich and full that they lend themselves to different viewpoints. The parables, like all our Lord's teachings, were given as the occasion arose. He did not group them into special classes. For our present study, we are suggesting a grouping according to the spiritual message.

We will begin with those parables that reveal what kind of a being God is, then we will go on to the question of what the response of the human heart should be toward such a God, and we will conclude with parables that touch on realms of spiritual truth and Christian service—service, prayer, and stewardship.

A Plan for Studying the Parables

This book is intended to help Bible readers study parables for themselves. Hopefully it will also prove interesting and helpful to those who wish to read another person's thinking about the message contained in a particular parable or to receive new light on the Word. It may be used for systematic study in the classroom or for more informal use in church education, as well as for individual study. No matter how it is used, the benefit derived from this volume will be in proportion to how much students follow the suggestions given here and then go on to dig into the subject for themselves.

Each lesson begins with questions that serve as preparation for the study that follows. Most students will not be able to give a complete answer to every question, but this should not cause discouragement. The purpose of these questions is to stimulate thinking, and the attempt to answer them will make the study all the more interesting.

Perhaps the reader will experience in some measure the joy of the businessman who exclaimed at the close of a Bible conference: "This week I have learned to walk!" He went on to explain that he had not been walking as much as he once had. Even when he needed to go around the corner, he would jump into his car. It had been that way with his Bible study, too. He had been hearing and reading what others said about the Bible. He had lost the wholesome habit of reading and interpreting it for himself.

This second-hand Bible study is the bane of many Christians. It leaves them dependent on some teacher whose interpretations come to have the authority of infallible truth.

No matter what may be thought of the interpretations suggested in this book, it is the earnest desire of the writer that this volume may help toward that most fascinating of all pursuits—the pursuit of truth through searching the Scriptures, the Word of God that has been given for everyone to read and to understand.

How to Use the Questions

The questions at the outset of each lesson are intended to stimulate the reader to think more about the parable before reading the study contained in the lesson. The review questions at the close of each lesson will help the reader to determine how much of the lesson has been mastered and will also stimulate discussion.

The best plan for readers is as follows: write out the answers to the preparation questions; read the lesson and review your answers to the preparation questions; then go on to answer the review questions from memory.

PART I

INTRODUCTORY MATERIAL

PREPARATION FOR LESSON 1

1. List the parables of our Lord that you can recall from memory.

2. What is a parable? Give what you think would be a good definition.

3. Read Matthew 13:1-9,18-23. This is the parable of the sower and the explanation given by our Lord. How does this illustrate your definition of a parable?

4. Read John 10:1-6. Would you call this a parable? What is the difference in form between this and the parable of the sower?

5. Luke 4:23 gives a "parable" in three words. Would you include this among the parables of our Lord? How is it similar to and how does it differ from what we usually call a parable?

Lesson 1

An Introductory Study

What Is a Parable?

A parable is an earthly story with a heavenly meaning. This brief definition is very familiar to most Christians. Like most brief sayings, it does not give as full or clear an idea of a topic as we would like, but it is helpful. Another definition with a helpful thought is: A parable is an outside story with an inside meaning.

The word *parable* is made up from two Greek words, *para* and *ballō*. The former means "alongside of," and the latter means "to put" or "to place" or "to throw." In a parable we put one thing alongside another in order to compare them.

Let us take as an illustration the first parable given in the New Testament—the parable of the sower. It is found in Matthew 13:3-8, Mark 4:3-8, and Luke 8:5-8. This is a story of sowing seed, with a meaning that relates to the sowing of the Word of God in the human heart. The sower sowing the seed, which falls on different kinds of soil, is put alongside the preaching or teaching of the spiritual seed, the Word of God, which enters the soil of human hearts.

A parable is only one form of figurative language used in the

Bible. Let us examine several other types of figurative language and note how each differs from the parable.

Fable

A fable is an unreal or imaginary story in which animals or inanimate objects talk and reason as if they were human beings. We are familiar with this form if we have read *Aesop's Fables*. But long before Aesop lived, Jotham told the fable that is recorded in Judges 9:7-20. Trees are here represented as going forth to choose a king to reign over them. Another fable in the Old Testament is found in 2 Kings 14:9-10, where Jehoash, the king of Israel, speaks of a thistle asking a cedar of Lebanon to give its daughter in marriage to the son of the thistle.

A parable differs from a fable in that the story within a parable does not contain anything unreal. It is not a true story, but it *is* true to life.

Simile and Metaphor

Two of the most familiar figures of speech are the simile and the metaphor.

A simile is the comparison of two unlike objects, with the sign of likeness directly expressed. "That man is like a lion" is an example of a simile because a man is not a lion. A beautiful simile is found in Isaiah 55:10-11, where the rain and the snow from heaven watering the earth is likened to the word that goes forth from God.

A metaphor is the putting together of two unlike objects, with the sign of likeness omitted. In a metaphor one thing is said to be the other. For example, "That man is a lion." Our Lord spoke of Herod as a "fox" (Luke 13:32), and this is another example of a metaphor. "This is my body" (Matt. 26:26) is a most notable metaphor because certain branches of the Christian church have decided that this is to be understood literally. This shows the importance of taking note of these figures of speech when we are interpreting the Bible.

What is the relation of a parable to a simile or a metaphor? A parable is sometimes called an extended simile. That is, when a comparison is expressed within the framework of an incident or a story, we call this a parable. For this reason some similes could also be called parables—that is, "parable-similes."

The most notable example is found in the closing words of our Lord in the Sermon on the Mount. The wise man who built his house on the rock and the foolish man who built his house on the sand are likened to the two kinds of hearers of His words. Most Bible teachers have called this a simile rather than a parable. However, it might well be considered a parable for it is certainly an extended simile.

Perhaps one reason it is not included in most lists of the parables is the statement in Matthew 13:3, "Then he told them many things in parables." The impression is given that this is the beginning of His teaching by parables. In speaking of a parable as an extended simile, we should bear in mind that this applies only when the simile deals with comparisons that might happen in actual life.

Allegory

When a metaphor is extended into a narrative, we call this an allegory. John Bunyan's *Pilgrim's Progress* is the most famous example of an allegory. Psalm 23 is the greatest of all allegories. In the Gospel of John we read the beautiful allegory of the vine and the branches (15:1-8). This passage begins, "I am the true vine, and my Father is the gardener." A parable, on the other hand, begins something like this: "The kingdom of heaven is like a mustard seed" (Matt. 13:31). Notice also that the spiritual message of an allegory is given along with the story, while in a parable the story is set off by itself and is complete in its own right.

Most commentators hold that John's Gospel contains no parables. The illustration of the sheep pen in John 1:1-6 is usually considered an allegory because the spiritual truth is *implied in* each sentence, though it is not directly stated as is the case of Psalm 2, and the vine and the branches. This description of the sheep pen may also be viewed as a parable according to our definition of the word—even though it does not record a specific happening. In an allegory each statement has a spiritual meaning. In a parable, as we shall see, the story may be taken as complete in itself, apart from the spiritual application. The greatest scholars have differed as to who is represented by "the watchman" in John 10:3. However, if we view this passage as a parable, it will not be necessary to give a specific spiritual application to the watchman.

Proverb

The proverb is another interesting figure of speech that should be noted in connection with the study of parables. A proverb gives in a few words an easily understood statement of generally accepted wisdom.

The original language of the New Testament has separate words for parable and proverb. However, there is some interchange between the words. For instance, in Luke 4:23 the word should be "parable" but some versions render it "proverb" because it is followed by a proverb. Likewise, in John 10:6 some versions use the word "parable" when the original called for "proverb"; but parable does seem to fit the sense of the passage better.

Listing the Parables

We see that there is a difference of opinion as to what should be called a parable. This explains why some passages are considered to be parables by some commentators but not by others. At the close of this volume the reader will find appendixes listing parabolic sayings and what we call parable-similes. The latter might well be called parables by another commentator; and, conversely, several of the passages that we classify as parables might be called parable-similes by others. Several of the sayings of John that we consider to be parabolic sayings are also listed at the back of this volume.

Old Testament Parables

There are many parables in Jewish literature outside the Bible, but they do not have the beauty and power of our Lord's parables. When we think of parables we think only of those that the Master Teacher spoke. We should, however, note that there are several parables in the Old Testament. The most familiar and beautiful is that of the ewe lamb, told by Nathan to convict David of his great sin. Here is our list of Old Testament parables: the ewe lamb (2 Sam. 12:1-4); the widow's two sons (2 Sam. 14:1-11); the escaped captive (1 Kings 20:35-40); the vineyard and grapes (Isa. 5:1-7); and the delivered city (Eccl. 9:14-15).

Three of the illustrations in Ezekiel are sometimes classed as parables: the eagles and the vine (17:3-10); the lion's whelps (19:2-9); and the boiling pot (24:3-5).

Defining the Word "Parable"

Here is our definition of *parable:* A parable is a brief story that is true to life, given for the purpose of teaching some spiritual truth.

A fuller definition is: A parable is a brief story or narrative drawn from human life or from nature, not relating to some actual event, but true to life and concerning something very familiar to the listeners, given for the purpose of teaching a spiritual truth.

When we say a parable is true to life, it does not mean that every incident in a parable is something that would happen in everyday life; but they *could* happen, and the situations are usually very familiar to the hearer.

How to Study a Parable

There are three steps in studying a parable.

First, study the three parts: the setting, the story, and the spiritual message, as given in the Scriptures.

Second, observe three principles in finding the central message:

1. Each parable has one, and only one, central message.
2. Each parable has a number of details that have a spiritual significance of their own, but all of these details also relate to the one central message.
3. Each parable has details that have no special spiritual significance.

Third, study the application or applications to our own life and service.

In the next lesson we will begin our study of the parables by using the story of the good Samaritan. We will see from our study of this parable how important it is to take note of the three steps outlined above if we are to understand the meaning of a parable.

REVIEW OF
THE INTRODUCTION
AND LESSON 1

1. Why, do you think, is it important to study our Lord's parables?

2. What is the difference between a parable and a simile? Give an example of a simile. What is a "parable-simile"?

3. Name five different forms of figurative language (including any figures of speech) used in the Bible. How do parables differ from each of these, and how are they related?

4. How does the derivation of the word *parable* help to explain what a parable is? Illustrate this meaning from the parable of the sower.

5. List the three principles presented in lesson 1 for discovering the central message of a parable.

PREPARATION FOR LESSON 2

Reading Lesson: Luke 10:25-37; Matthew 19:16-22; 22:34-40

1. What is the setting of this parable?

2. Why did this lawyer ask Jesus who his neighbor was?

3. What idea did the Jews have of who their neighbor was? (Read Leviticus 19:18.) What idea did the Pharisees have? (Read John 7:49.)

4. Where else in Scripture are two short statements given as a summary of the law?

5. Do you think this parable teaches that the way to get eternal life is to do kind deeds?

Lesson 2

The Good Samaritan

Luke 10:30-35

We have seen that each parable has three parts: (1) the occasion, or setting; (2) the story itself; and (3) the spiritual message. We will study the parable of the good Samaritan with the special purpose of identifying these three parts.

The Setting (Luke 10:25-29)

Why did our Lord tell this parable? To answer that question we must look at the setting. The occasion for this parable is the question of a lawyer, "And who is my neighbor?" (Luke 10:29). The parable is given to answer that question.

But we should read the context in order to get the full setting. What do we need to know in order to understand the setting? We should know what "an expert in the law," or a lawyer is. We want to know what was in his mind when he asked about how to inherit eternal life, and why he asked the question "Who is my neighbor?"

There are two interesting parallel passages that we have read in preparation for this lesson: Matthew 19:16-22, the story of the rich young man, and Matthew 22:34-40, the record of the lawyer who asked the Lord which was the great commandment of the law.

25

The rich young man asked the Lord what he must do to inherit eternal life. His question was earnest and sincere, and he wanted light for himself personally. But the lawyer in Luke 10 "stood up to test Jesus," and his question was not earnest and sincere (v. 25). In the case of the rich young man, he also was tested on this command to love his neighbor as himself. He failed, and because he was an earnest seeker he went away sorrowful. This lawyer was evidently thinking of it all in a cold, impersonal way.

A lawyer was a student and interpreter of the Old Testament; he was one who told the people how to apply the law to the details of their lives. Most of them were enemies of the Lord. They were also called "scribes," or teachers of the law (cf. Matt. 22:35; Mark 12:28). Both the Pharisees and the Sadducees had lawyers within their ranks.

We may learn what the spirit of those lawyers was by reading the terrible rebukes that our Lord pronounced against them (Luke 11:45-52; Matt. 5:20; 23:1-39). They were hypocrites who paid attention to outward forms of religion, but in their hearts they had no humility nor any desire to know God. They weighed down men, especially the poor, with heavy burdens and had no interest in helping them.

The lawyer mentioned in Mark 12:28-34 is an exception; the Lord said that he was not far from the kingdom. In Luke 10 it is remarkable that when our Lord asked this lawyer what was written in the law about eternal life he answered by giving Him two commandments—to love God with all your heart and your neighbor as yourself. These are the same commandments our Lord quoted to the lawyer in Mark 12. This shows that the lawyers knew the teaching of the Old Testament and that the two commandments that summed up the law— supreme love for God and love for man—had been made very plain to them.

But we read that the lawyer wanted to justify himself. He

knew that he had broken these commandments and, therefore, he was not just before God. Instead of humbly seeking God's way of forgiveness and salvation, with a proud heart he refused to confess his sinfulness. He sought to justify himself, or prove that he was right before the law.

What did he mean when he asked, "And who is my neighbor?" If we turn to Leviticus 19:18 where we have the command "Love your neighbor as yourself," we find that this refers to "one of your people," to a fellow Jew. The Jews, and especially the scribes and Pharisees, interpreted this very literally as applying to their own people only. We recall that Peter, even after the outpouring of the Holy Spirit on the day of Pentecost, needed a special revelation from God before he would go to the household of Cornelius, a Gentile. Very deep-seated, then, was this wrong idea.

If Christ had tried to teach directly against the lawyer's idea of who his neighbor was, it would have meant a complete upsetting of the ideas of not only His enemies but also of His disciples. The time was not right for them to hear or understand such truth. This, we shall see, is one of the great reasons for teaching through parables. Also it is one of the reasons our Lord answered the lawyer's question about eternal life by referring him to the law. He always dealt with souls just where they were and sought to lead them out of the error that darkened them into spiritual truth.

This lawyer might have argued that he *did* love his neighbor, defining a neighbor as a fellow Jew who believed as he did and who treated him lovingly. For the Pharisees did not even count every Jew as a real neighbor. They drew the lines closer about themselves (John 7:49).

We have briefly considered the setting of this parable. We may also call this getting the historical background. We will find as we go on that it is important to learn all we can about this setting. Although we may get real blessing from the parable without going fully into all these matters, we will miss much of its significance by not putting ourselves back, in so far as this is possible, into the time when it was first told. This is our aim in studying the setting—to put ourselves into the position of those to whom our Lord first spoke the parable. Now we are ready for the story itself.

The Story (Luke 10:30-35)

Few things are more important in understanding a parable than to study the story, all by itself and apart from what the spiritual meaning may be. Let us first make several observations about this story.

1. The story is remarkably brief. How long does it take you to read it? In the original language there are 143 words. What a story to be packed into that space!

2. The story is vivid and full of action. Every sentence is a picture. It grips the attention of children; they can see the thing happening.

3. The story is full of human interest. Both in their time and in ours, people are fascinated by robbers, the adventures of a traveler, the fate of a man left half-dead, and the way he is treated by various passers-by.

4. The story had startling and unexpected features of vital concern to all of the people who heard it. When this unusual Teacher from Galilee mentioned a priest, the common people would listen very carefully to what He had to say. They knew these men were far from what priests should be, and yet they feared them and dared not criticize. It was the same with the mention of Levites, who, like the priests, should have set the example of godliness and neighborliness. But the climax was the mention of a Samaritan and the fact that he is the center of attention in the story.

To us a "Samaritan" is one who is like the man who comes to the rescue in this parable. This shows the tremendous power of these 143 words. Samaritan is now linked with "good," and we even have hospitals with that name. But to the Jews, the word *Samaritan* represented everything that was low and despised. To contrast a Jewish priest with a Samaritan and make the Samaritan good and the priest evil, would enrage the Pharisees. It must have caused all of our Lord's hearers to gasp at its daring.

5. The story has one central theme. In a perfect story there will always be one central theme, the action will work up to a climax, and usually there is one person who stands out. The theme of this story is contained in the title always given to it: the good Samaritan. All centers in him. The purpose is not to make the robbers prominent, nor the innkeeper, nor even the wounded traveler. The priest and the Levite have an important part in the story, but their part has meaning only in connection with what the good Samaritan does.

6. The story compels moral assent. That is, all the listeners will be, indeed, *must* be, in full sympathy with the central character of the story. They must also be in full agreement with the point that the storyteller has in mind. There are stories that cause differences of opinion and divided sympathies in the audience, but in this story no one would applaud the priest or the Levite and condemn the good Samaritan.

7. Some knowledge of the historical background is necessary in order to appreciate the story fully. Because it is a story full of human interest, the meaning will be clear to men of all ages. There are details of the story that are always with us— robbers, the innkeeper, the selfish travelers, and the merciful and generous man. But there are other details that we must learn by studying the times. We must study about Jerusalem, Jericho, priests, Levites, and Samaritans.

We have seen the importance of putting ourselves back into the times of our Lord in order to understand the setting of the parable. So also in order to know the story fully, we should try to put ourselves in the shoes of those who first heard it. We have already noted the startling effect it would have on the people to speak of a priest, a Levite, and a Samaritan in the same story; to know who these three characters are, therefore, adds to our understanding of the story.

We can get much information from what the Bible says about priests and Levites and from our Lord's experience with the Samaritan woman told in John 4. Other interesting material may be gathered from Bible dictionaries. Jericho is only incidental to the story, but it is interesting that the road from Jericho to Jerusalem, about twenty miles long, was often dangerous to travel. We may also recall the history of Jericho: it was the first city to be destroyed by the Israelites under Joshua; a curse was pronounced on the man who rebuilt it (Josh. 6:26); and this curse was carried out on a man named Hiel in the days of wicked King Ahab (1 Kings 16:34).

The seven observations above help us to appreciate the story and prepare us for the principles that we must keep in mind when we look for the spiritual meaning. We will see that these observations hold true of nearly all of our Lord's parables.

The Spiritual Message (Luke 10:36-37)

We said earlier that in a parable the story is alongside of the spiritual message. The more clearly we know and appreciate the story, therefore, the more fully we will understand the spiritual meaning. The spiritual meaning should be as definite, as clear cut, as full of interest, as briefly put, and as simply understood as the story itself.

In the case of the good Samaritan, notice in how few words the application is given. First a question by our Lord: "Which of these three do you think was a neighbor to the man who fell into the hands of robbers?" (Luke 10:36). Then the lawyer answers, illustrating that the story compels moral assent. The lawyer had to give the answer our Lord wanted; there was no other answer to be given. He said: "The one who had mercy on him" (v. 37). Then came the brief but pregnant personal appeal of the message: "Go and do likewise."

It is from these words that we are to get the spiritual message our Lord intended to teach with this parable. What was it? How would you express it in one sentence?

In studying the story we found that there was one central theme. In finding the spiritual meaning we will see that the most important principle to be kept in mind is that there is one central message in the parable, *and only one.* There may also be several spiritual messages, or several truths, just as there are several details in the story; but these are not separate or independent truths. They are all related to the one central message. The parable is perfect in that every important detail of the story does have a spiritual meaning and has a part in making vivid the central message.

In the setting we found that the parable was given to answer the question, "Who is my neighbor?" So it should be very evident that the message to be taught is, Who is my neighbor? What answer does the parable give? Probably nine out of ten Christians, and in some cases ten out of ten, will answer that the neighbor is the man in need of your help, as the good Samaritan recognized the man robbed and wounded as his neighbor. However, this answer misses the point of the parable. This shows the importance of the method of studying the parables that we are following. It is quite true that the man in need *is* our neighbor. But is that what our Lord said, and is that the point of the parable? Note the question again, "Which of these three do you think was a neighbor?"

It was not the wounded man who is the neighbor in the parable; the good Samaritan is the neighbor. And that is the point of the parable and the answer to the lawyer. He was asking that *neighbor* be defined so that he could know the limits of his obligation to love others. Christ turned the whole question around and taught him, and us: It is not a question of how many others are neighbors to you but of whether you are a neighbor, with a heart of love, going out to every person you may help.

Here was a story full of human interest and with which every listener had to agree. Yet mark this tremendous fact: No one who heard the story and the application had any idea of how revolutionary the teaching was. We take the teaching of this parable as a commonplace truth. But those who knew most about the true God in the days of our Lord—the leaders of the Jews and those who followed Jesus Christ as their Messiah—had an idea of neighbor and of love for man that was the very opposite of the truth of the parable. We speak today of revolutionary teaching. But here is the marvel of our Lord's parables: His quiet, simple words, spoken as an occasion arose, turned people's ideas upside down.

The Personal Application

Even in our day, do we dare to face the real meaning of being a neighbor? How does this apply to our responsibility to the heathen? to race relationships? to fraternities of various kinds? to Christians in other denominations?

We will find most of our Lord's parables—we may say all of them—taught truths that were the very opposite of the thought of the natural mind. If this is so, then we should be careful not to pass off as commonplace, and therefore unimportant, the teaching of a parable. It is the commonplace truth that is the truth of transcendent importance.

For our present study we may state the central message of the parable thus, using the word *Christian*, which of course was not known in those days: A Christian is a neighbor, and as such is to be always ready to serve those in need.

No statement of the teaching, of course, can take the place of the parable itself, for every part of it adds to this central message. The fact that a priest and Levite passed by not only shows what human nature is capable of, it also shows that being a religious leader is no guarantee that the heart will be right. The Samaritan's actions show that love is expressed in practical ways and that it meets the need fully. The help that the Samaritan gave sprang from the love in his heart; it was compassion that moved him, not self-interest. The fact that he was a Samaritan shows that God is no respecter of persons. He does not look at a man's race or his face or his outward appearance but on his heart. Thus we see that every important detail of the story does have a spiritual significance.

Notice now that there are other details that belong to the story and are necessary for its completeness but that have no special spiritual significance. It is not necessary to search for a specific meaning in the two silver coins, or in the oil and wine that was poured on the wounds, or in the Samaritan setting the wounded man on his own donkey, except as all these details show the practical expression of compassion and unselfish service.

According to one interpretation of this parable, the good Samaritan represents our Lord Himself; the wounded traveler, the sinful human race; the priest and Levite, the moral and ceremonial law; the inn, the church; and the two silver coins, the two sacraments, or the Old and New Testaments. Others have spoken of the good Samaritan's going away and returning as referring to our Lord's return and the two silver coins representing prayer and Bible study on which we feed till His return. If such interpretations are allowed, then it is evident that parables can be made to mean almost anything the ingenuity of the student can force upon them. But if the spiritual message is as simple and clear and beautiful as the story itself, we can find principles of interpretation that will save us from going astray.

A more serious and more plausible misinterpretation of the parable is that which suggests that eternal life is to be won by charitable deeds. If we hold to our principle of seeking one central message, we see that our Lord was not here suggesting that good deeds would win salvation. He was not dealing with that question here. The relation of the central message in this parable to the question of eternal life is an important one, and this will be taken up when we refer to this parable again in lesson 6.

Meanwhile we may state the truth of the parable of the good Samaritan with a summary statement: A Christian is a neighbor, and as such is to be always ready to serve those in need. This attitude does not save him but is the fruit of his salvation; it does not win him eternal life but is the evidence that he has eternal life.

REVIEW OF LESSON 2

1. What does the setting of this parable show us of the need of both the lawyer and the disciples for Christ's teaching about a neighbor?

2. What is the central teaching of this parable?

3. Suppose that you had just heard this parable. How would you report this story to Jewish people of that day who had not heard it?

4. Give an example from your own experience of the lack of this kind of neighborliness.

5. Give an example of someone who has been a real neighbor.

PART II

PARABLES
OF THE
FATHER'S HEART

PREPARATION FOR LESSON 3

Reading Lesson: Luke 15:1-10; Matthew 18:1-14

1. Why would the story of the lost sheep appeal to people of that day?

2. What is the difference in the setting of the parable of the lost sheep in Luke and the setting of the same story in Matthew?

3. Do you think Luke 14 has any relation to these parables? That is, can we understand the setting any better from a study of this chapter?

4. Who were the "tax collectors and sinners," and what was their relation to the Pharisees?

5. What was the relation of Jesus to these two groups?

The Lost Sheep
The Lost Coin

Luke 15:4-6; Luke 15:9-10

A study of parables could begin with the parables of the kingdom in Matthew 13, especially since they appear first in the New Testament. But most beginning Bible students will find it difficult to grasp the full significance of these kingdom parables without a rather extended study of the first twelve chapters of Matthew and their relation to portions of the Old Testament.

We begin, then, on the more familiar ground of the three parables in Luke 15, together with the parable of the lost sheep as given in Matthew 18.

THE LOST SHEEP IN LUKE

The Setting (Luke 15:1-2)

Why is it of such importance to study the setting of a parable? We should, so far as possible, put ourselves back into the time and place in which our Lord spoke the parables. In this case there is a group of three parables, all of them having the same setting. This setting is given by Luke in the first two verses of the chapter.

There is mention of "tax collectors and sinners" coming to Jesus, and of "Pharisees and the teachers of the law" murmuring. We have already referred to the picture of scribes and Pharisees in the Scriptures. The tax collectors gathered the public taxes, under Rome. They were despised by their fellow Jews as outcasts, both because of the hatred of the Roman yoke and because of the dishonesty of many of them. Taxes were in many cases farmed out, and the collector took for himself all he could above the amount to be paid to the officer above him. Our Lord's reference to the tax collectors in Matthew 5:46 suggests something of their character.

With this knowledge of the people in these parables, we should seek to get a good understanding of the scene. A vivid picture is given of large numbers of tax collectors and sinners eager to hear the Lord Jesus. Standing off as criticizing and fault-finding observers are the Pharisees and scribes, murmuring that "this man," as they contemptuously refer to our Lord, receives sinners and eats with them.

The marginal references in your Bible may refer to Matthew 9:10-13, where the Pharisees ask the disciples why Jesus ate with tax collectors and sinners. Their question drew two striking answers from our Lord. The first was a proverb or parabolic saying, "It is not the healthy who need a doctor, but the sick." The second was a direct statement, "I have not come to call the righteous, but sinners."

These verses shed light on the setting of the three parables in Luke, as do many other passages of the Gospels that speak of the constant conflict between our Lord and the Pharisees. The Pharisees and scribes prided themselves on being believers in God and interpreters of His character. Here, in Luke 15, they are boldly suggesting that Jesus is not to be trusted as a teacher and that God would not approve of what He is doing.

Thus, while the setting is given in these two verses, the more fully we understand the whole ministry of our Lord, the more fully we can appreciate these parables. Luke 14 is especially helpful in more fully understanding the setting. In the parable of the great banquet recorded there, our Lord gives the message of going out into the roads and country lanes to call men of all classes to come because those first invited refused to come. This corresponds to the Pharisees who refused the invitation and to the tax collectors and sinners in chapter 15.

The parables are told, then, as our Lord's answer to the murmuring of the scribes and Pharisees. And what an answer!

The Story (Luke 15:4-6)

Read the story again and write down the characteristics you notice. It is very important to get into the habit of appreciating the story itself, considered as a story, without reference to its spiritual meaning. To appreciate this story observe, first, its literal meaning to the people of that day and, second, its figurative meaning to the godly Jews and to Christians who know something of what the Bible means when it uses sheep to represent God's people.

This story does not touch on the everyday life of twentieth-century Americans in the same way that it did on the people of Jesus' day. But it was true to life for the Jews, and to appreciate this we must know that shepherds of those days called their sheep by name and tenderly cared for their every need.

Those who have time for an extended study of the relationship between a shepherd and his sheep may read again Psalm 23, Ezekiel 34, Jeremiah 23, and other Old Testament references to Jehovah as the true Shepherd of His people. All of these prepare the way for the revelation of the Lord Jesus as the Good Shepherd in John 10. "We are his people, and the sheep of his pasture" (Ps. 100:3). "We all, like sheep, have gone astray . . . and the LORD has laid on him the iniquity of us all" (Isa. 53:6). Notice that sheep may represent lost sinners, gone astray, as well as God's children.

To sum up some of the characteristics of the story itself, we note: its brevity; its vivid details; its personal appeal to what is familiar to the hearers; its simplicity; its human interest, especially to those who are familiar with the subject; its appeal that compels moral assent to the point of the story; its true-to-life character; and its completeness.

After noting the characteristics of the story, ask yourself what its central point is, *as a story*. The focus of the story is evidently the attitude of the shepherd toward one sheep out of a hundred, an attitude that leads him to go to all lengths till he finds the sheep. The climax of the story is his joy at finding the sheep. First he rejoices as he puts the sheep on his shoulders, and then he shares this joy with his friends and neighbors.

The Spiritual Message (Luke 15:7)

Before going on with the study, write out your own statement of what the central message of this parable is. You will notice how important is the study of the setting and of the story itself if we are to appreciate the spiritual message. The third point under our first rule for the study of parables is to study the spiritual message as given in the Scriptures. In this case our Lord Himself tells us this in verse 7.

Now we are ready to observe the three principles in finding the message, and ask first: What is the one central message of the parable? Here are some answers that have been given:

- God's seeking for the lost sinner
- God's love for men
- God's care for a single soul
- God's compassion for anyone in need

All of these are precious truths and are included in the message of the parable, but none of them encompass the spiritual message. Notice that the message as given by our Lord centers attention on the joy in heaven over one sinner who repents, as represented by the joy of the shepherd in finding his sheep. This joy is evidently the heart of the message.

Furthermore, the central theme of the story must also be the central theme of the spiritual message. The theme of the story is the shepherd's attitude toward a single lost sheep. The central spiritual message, therefore, is the revelation of the heavenly Father's heart toward one lost soul who repents. Our Lord is saying to the Pharisees, "My attitude toward these tax collectors and sinners is a revelation of the Father's heart. He is filled with joy at each one of these sinners who is coming to Me."

Notice how this central message of the Father's heart of love is made vivid by the details of the story and its setting. It is an individual love, a heart of love that goes out toward one. It is a personal love, beautifully portrayed in paintings that depict sheep on the shoulders of the shepherd. It is a love that loves to the end and goes to any sacrifice. It is a love for the lost one, the one who has strayed. Finally, it is a love that expresses itself in great joy that the lost has been found—joy because it matters greatly to the loving Father that we repent, and joy because our happiness is wrapped up in coming back to the fold.

This is a love that is the opposite of proud Pharisees, who are sneering at the tax collectors and sinners who are repenting. They can understand neither the love that yearns for the lost nor the repentance that leads to a change in the sinner's heart, making him lovely in the eyes of God.

Because the parables of our Lord use many details to focus on the central message, it is natural that men should seek a spiritual meaning in every detail and thus go astray in understanding the parables. Here are some *false* views that may be mistakenly drawn from the parable:

- The sheep was not morally responsible for being lost, and therefore neither is the sinner.
- The shepherd sought till he found. So God seeks till He finds, and the responsibility is all His. The sheep is sure to be found.
- The sheep was once in the fold. Therefore he represents not the lost sinner but a Christian who has strayed.
- Ninety-nine were left. Therefore there are one in a hundred who will stray and ninety-nine who do not need to be saved.
- The ninety-nine were left in the wilderness. God leaves the ninety-nine to take care of themselves while He seeks the lost.

These wrong interpretations show the importance of our third principle: there are several details that belong to the story but have no definite spiritual application. How can we know which details do not have spiritual meaning? First, through holding closely to our one central message and all that is related to it. The purpose of this parable is to show God's heart of love for one lost soul. It has nothing to do with the plan of how God saves, nor the proportion of saved and lost, nor the responsibility of lost sinners, nor God's relation to those who are saved.

There is one important detail we have not mentioned. This passage says there is joy in heaven (which is God's joy) over one sinner, more than over ninety-nine who need no repentance. Here we have a significant fact about most of the parables: they teach by contrast. The Father's heart is shown in contrast with the Pharisees' heart. The sinner who repents is shown in contrast with the righteous who need no repentance.

The question arises, Are these righteous the Christians who have already repented or are they the Pharisees who say they need no repentance? Our Lord's statement in Matthew 9:13,

"I have not come to call the righteous, but sinners," suggests that the parable of the lost sheep is referring, as do many other passages in the Gospels, to those who consider themselves not to need repentance.

We know from other Scripture that there is none righteous, that all need to repent, and we also know that our Lord, by a figure of speech, refers to the self-righteous in their own terms as "righteous" who need no repentance. It seems clear, then, that as the lost sheep represents the tax collector and sinner, so the ninety-nine represent the Pharisees who thought they needed no repentance.

The Personal Application

If our Father has such a heart, what does it mean for us? This answer must be given by each one individually. If we really understand something of this parable, it will give us a vivid sense of the fact that we have been lost sheep, needing to repent. It will assure us of the wonder of God's personal and individual love for us. And it will teach us to seek deliverance from the heart of the Pharisee—not only from his self-righteousness but also from his lack of joy over sinners who repent.

If we have a heart like God's, we will also rejoice greatly over every sinner who repents. And it will follow that our chief concern in life will be seeking and finding the lost and bringing them back to the fold, thus increasing the joy of our Father's heart.

THE LOST SHEEP IN MATTHEW

The same story of the lost sheep is told in Matthew 18: 12-13. But the setting is quite different. The message as given by our Lord is also different.

The Setting (Matt. 18:1-11)

Read this passage to discover the setting of the parable and the differences between it and the setting in Luke 15. Then read and notice how the message of the parable differs from that given in Luke. This is a splendid illustration of the fact that a parable is not the story alone but the story in its setting. It shows also the importance of understanding the setting and the teaching intended by the Master.

At the very time when our Lord is seeking to reveal to His disciples His approaching death on the cross and to have them understand the spirit of the cross, they are disputing as to which of them should be greatest. They are interested in who is to have first place in the kingdom that they expect soon to be inaugurated. In answer to such questions, our Lord calls a little child and teaches the disciples about the necessity of becoming as little children in order to enter the kingdom of heaven.

Then He goes on to speak of young believers as little children and of the terrible sin of causing one of them to stumble. The "little ones" whose angels always behold the face of the Father doubtless include the little children themselves and also young believers. Then follows the parable of the lost sheep.

The Spiritual Message (Matt. 18:14)

What is its message? Again it is the revelation of the heart of the Father. But this time it is not the heart of the Father toward those tax collectors and sinners who were coming to Jesus to hear His word and to repent. It is the heart of the Father toward the "little ones." "In the same way your Father in heaven is not willing that any of these little ones should be lost" (Matt. 18:14).

In Luke the thought centers on the sinner who has gone

astray from righteousness, and the heart of God goes out to him in yearning love. In Matthew the thought is of the Father's tender love toward every child. He does not want a single one to go astray. This is a beautiful parable, with the same central message of the Father's heart of love, applied to two kinds of sinners—the little children who are sinners by nature and who will go off into sin and on to destruction if they are not saved and the sinners who have wandered far off into sin.

As the parable in Luke is a solemn warning against the attitude of the self-righteous Pharisee, the parable in Matthew is a warning against those who would cause a little one to stumble and against the proud person who does not recognize the need of becoming as a little child and does not put the value on little children that God puts on them.

We have seen that what our Lord said ran counter to what the world thought about who our neighbor is. What he said also ran counter to what the world thought about tax collectors and sinners and little children—both the little ones themselves and the childlike believers.

THE LOST COIN

The second parable in Luke 15 begins, "Or suppose a woman has ten silver coins." This shows that the same truth presented in the parable of the lost sheep is to be taught through another illustration. The setting, then, is the same. The story, again, is true to life as they knew it but not as we know it today.

To understand this story we need to appreciate the joy that would attend the discovery of a lost coin. Also we should realize that these ten coins are probably not simply so many pieces of money, the loss of one of which would not be a serious matter. Evidently the ten were important either as an heirloom or as a prized collection. Even in this century women in Palestine have worn their total wealth on their headdresses, in the form of coins or jewelry.

In this parable the thing that is lost is an inanimate object. Therefore it does not deal with the question of the sinner's responsibility. Again the central message is the value of the lost soul in the sight of the God who is love and His great joy over the sinner who repents. Neither in this parable nor in that of the lost sheep is the thought of repentance brought out, for the message concerns the Father's attitude as revealed in these homely illustrations.

A beautiful touch is added in the statement of the spiritual lesson; the joy is "in the presence of the angels of God." It is the Father's joy, expressed before the angels and shared by them, even as the friends and neighbors came to rejoice with the woman.

REVIEW OF LESSON 3

1. Where else in Scripture are sheep prominently mentioned with the purpose of giving spiritual teaching? What do sheep represent here?

2. What is the central message of the parable of the lost sheep in Matthew? How does this differ from the central message of this same parable in Luke?

3. What is the central message of the parable of the lost coin?

4. Which details in the stories of the lost sheep and of the lost coin have spiritual significance?

5. Name several qualities of our heavenly Father that are shown in these parables.

PREPARATION FOR LESSON 4

Reading Lesson: Luke 15:1-32

1. What are some things in the story that are different from present-day life, that is, things we could understand better by knowing the historical background?

2. Why is the younger son in the parable called lost? Does he repent as a sinner or as a Christian who has gone astray?

3. Does this parable deal with the matter of how men are saved?

4. Whom does the older brother represent and what spiritual teaching is there in his exchange with his father?

5. Can we enter into the experience of the lost son if we have never been involved in the same sort of sins?

Lesson 4

The Lost Son

Luke 15:11-32

The parables of the lost sheep and the lost coin are in a sense preparatory to the incomparable parable of the lost son. This story has been engraved on the heart of humanity as an unforgettable picture of sin and its consequences and of the Father's love for a straying child.

The Setting (Luke 15:1-2)

It is significant that no spiritual message is added to the story of the lost son as there is in the case of the lost sheep and the lost coin. The story itself, in combination with the setting, carries the tremendous message. The setting is the same as that for the preceding parables of the group.

We should try to appreciate the feelings of the tax collectors and sinners as they listened to this story of the father and his two sons. And what were the thoughts of the proud and self-righteous Pharisees who could not help but listen eagerly to the story that portrays their own hearts as well as the heart of God? Our Lord loves the Pharisees as well as the tax collectors and would, if possible, win them from their sinful attitude.

The Story (Luke 15:11-32)

This story is so familiar to us that we have probably never stopped to ask why it has such power. Read it aloud and note how little time it takes. Then try to find words that could be omitted. Every sentence is a picture, and the story is vivid—full of action and human interest. It is true to life in the deepest sense. Although we may not be familiar with some of the customs, the essentials of this story are timeless for its subject is human nature and sinfulness.

What are some features of the story that become clearer when we know the customs of that time? The dividing of the father's estate was perhaps not a common thing, but it was altogether possible. The older brother would receive two thirds of the estate, the younger brother a third. The "fattened calf," the best robe and the ring, the feasting and the dancing all fit into the life that would be very familiar to our Lord's listeners. Famine and the feeding of swine, the lowest level to which a Jewish lad could fall, were also familiar to those who heard this parable.

In studying the characteristics of the story, note how it differs from that of the lost sheep and the lost coin. Here we have the lost son, a sinner who recognizes his sin and repents. Here we have a joy that must have sounded an infinitely deeper note than the joy of the shepherd who found his sheep or of the woman who found her coin.

We may also notice that the lost sheep and the lost coin were diligently sought after till they were found. Here the father does not seek the son. He doubtless knew where he was; the older brother knew what his brother was doing. In any case, the father could not bring back his son as the shepherd brought back the sheep; he waited with longing until the son repented. Human will, which cannot be forced, is a factor in this story. In this parable there is one who does not share in the joy at the finding of the lost.

Remember that we are here considering the story itself and are not dealing with the spiritual message. In fact, in this parable the story itself contains spiritual teaching, for it deals with human sin and repentance. For this reason it is all the more important to keep distinct the story and its message, for in this way we get the true relation between them.

This parable, probably more than any other, has formed the text for many sermons. Perhaps this is because the story lends itself to so many lessons on life.

A young man tired of the humdrum life of home, sudden wealth, a distant country, wild living, lost wealth and lost friends, famine, shame, the memory of home and its comforts and love, repentance and return—how many thousands of times has this story been lived out in every land, and how many thousands of earnest appeals to repent have been based on this story? Because it is so rich and full, it is all the more important to discover the central theme of the story and thus learn what the central spiritual message is. In this case we will study the central theme of the story in connection with the spiritual message.

The Spiritual Message (Luke 15:11-32)

In no other parable is it more important to observe our three principles of interpretation. Let us notice some of the incorrect interpretations of this parable that have resulted from neglecting these principles.

The parable of the lost son has been a favorite passage for teachers within the church who preach a "different gospel." These teachers present the lost son as a picture of the gospel. There is not a word in the parable, they say, about the blood of Christ, nor about the atonement He made for sin, nor about the new birth. All that a sinner needs to do is to repent of his sin as did the lost son and decide to return to God. God will receive him with forgiveness and joy as the father did his son.

Those who hold this view go on to say that there is no suggestion in the parable of the work of the Holy Spirit. There is no mention of the father seeking his son or trying to persuade him to repent and return. Neither is there any restitution for the wrongs done, any punishment for the sin, nor satisfaction given the father for the sin against him.

If this parable is a picture of sin and salvation, there seems to be a foundation for this new "gospel." Although those who interpret the parable in this way usually pride themselves on being "scientific" in their treatment of the Bible, we notice here a complete departure from the central principle in interpreting parables, namely, that they are given to teach one central message and one only.

This parable has nothing to do with the question of how God solved the problem of sin through the death of Christ. Neither does it deal with the work of the Holy Spirit, God's part in seeking after men, or the need of regeneration. In the same way, it does not give teaching on the Incarnation, or on the deity of Christ, or the Resurrection, though all of these are essential to God's plan of redemption. It has one central teaching, and the many rich details are vitally related to this central truth.

There are also details that are not intended to convey a spiritual truth. Many of the facts about the relation of the father and his sons would not apply to the relation of God and men because a human father is not God. The story is a natural human story. We are to gather from it the one thing our Lord intended to teach.

But the enemies of the gospel are not alone in mistreating this parable. These same methods are used by friends of the gospel. One noted teacher has said this parable teaches that once a man is saved he can never be lost. Although he may wander into sin, he is sure to return. The son in the parable was a son even in his sin. So, we are told, the child of God who wanders away into sin is still a son and is sure to repent and return. If this is the teaching, does this parable have nothing to do with lost sinners? Were the tax collectors and sinners who came to Christ all children of God who had wandered away and were returning?

Another well-known teacher, commenting on the lost son, dwelt on the truth that if he had not repented and returned he would have been lost eternally.

A third teacher, when asked which of these two interpretations was correct, suggested that both were true and we might well believe that the parable included both teachings.

It is, of course, true that the eternal suffering of the impenitent and the eternal safety of believers are very precious truths revealed in Scripture, but this parable has nothing to do with such matters. It is not dealing with the fate of the impenitent nor with the position of a sinning Christian, any more than it is dealing with the truth of the Atonement, or the work of the Holy Spirit, or God's sovereignty.

To arrive at the central truth, we ask first: What is the central theme of the story? There are three main characters in the story: the father, the younger son, and the older brother. But there are not three separate stories about these characters. There is one story. The interest centers on the younger son. But notice that his wild life is not the climax or objective of the story. The result of that kind of life is an important feature, but this is not the central theme. His repentance is not the climax. Evidently all of these details point to the reception that the father gives the penitent son.

Why, then, is the older brother introduced? What is his part in the story? His character is sketched for us in a few words, and we get a glimpse of his life through the years. But observe that he is introduced only in connection with his relation to the central theme of the story: his attitude toward his brother in contrast to his father's attitude, and also the father's treatment of him revealing the father's attitude toward the older brother.

What one theme gathers together all of these details? Is it not the attitude of the father's heart? The father, then, is the real hero of the story, speaking in literary terms.

When we come to the spiritual message intended by our Lord, this central theme becomes more evident, for we have the setting to guide us. Notice that the setting of the lost son may well include the two parables that have gone before, the lost sheep and the lost coin, as well as the opening verses of the chapter. The central truth of the parable is the heavenly Father's heart of love toward an undeserving sinner, expressed in his great joy at his repentance and expressed also in his grief at the attitude that does not share this joy.

In the story, the wayward son deserves nothing from the father. He has received all his inheritance and has wasted it in the worst forms of sin. He has received his "wages." The wages of sin is death, and he was dead. He hopes that his father will receive him as a hired servant. He is given the welcome of a king—the best his father has.

The older brother pictures the awful character of the sin of his brother—"this son of yours," as he calls him, "who has squandered your property with prostitutes." The father is not minimizing the sin. He says to his son—"this brother of yours" was "dead" and "lost."

The father in the story represents the heavenly Father. The younger son represents the tax collectors and sinners who were coming to Jesus. The older brother undoubtedly represents the scribes and Pharisees who murmured at Christ's receiving sinners.

We should remember, however, that the father represents God in the revelation of his heart of love and not in every detail of his relation to his sons. The younger son represents the repentant sinner, and the fact that he is a son in the story does not give any teaching about becoming a child of God through the new birth. The sheep in the story of the lost sheep does not mean that the repentant sinner is an animal with four legs. In the same way, the son in the story is a son because this is a story of a father and his two sons. The details of the story must be kept distinct from the spiritual truth it presents.

The older brother is one of the most remarkable features of the parable. Is not our Lord appealing to these Pharisees to change their attitude? The older brother is typical of the Jews as a whole, just as the younger brother is typical of many of the Gentiles. But each is also a picture of the natural heart of every man. These two applications of the truth do not mean there are two truths.

What is the argument of the older brother? He stayed home through the years and never transgressed a commandment of his father's, yet the father never treated him with such feasting and joy. This was exactly the attitude of the Pharisees who were watching Jesus so closely. They had not sinned against God. That is, they had not sinned as the tax collectors had. This son, according to his own standard of outward righteousness, obeyed the father's commandments. The Jews also claimed they obeyed God's law. But in pointing to his obedience, the older son was grieving his father and resisting his earnest entreaties to come into the house and share the joy. This was also what the Pharisees were doing. They claimed to obey the law of God as given through Moses, and they were rejecting Jehovah Himself and resisting His pleading and entreaties.

The older son was self-righteous, proud, and joyless. We ask, Was he saved? The parable is not dealing with the question of whether or not he was saved. It is showing us the heart of God. And what was His heart toward the Pharisee or toward anyone who claims to be in His house? What is His attitude toward the repentant sinner after he is saved and takes up his abode in the Father's house?

This parable gives a startling answer: "My son, . . . you are always with me, and everything I have is yours." Read John 3:35, 16:15, and Romans 8:32 and see this wonderful truth in the light of the parable—the truth that God's love toward His own is expressed by giving them all that He has. He does this by giving us Christ, and in this present time He gives us the Holy Spirit to take of the things of Christ and reveal them to us.

With this great central message before us, we are able to see how all the details center in this truth, and we shall not try to seek some hidden meaning in the ring, the fattened calf, the best robe, and the sandals, except as these are the natural expression of the purpose to treat the son as his beloved. So the sinner who comes to the Father in Christ's name receives the best the Father has.

The Personal Application

No one can understand the real message of the parable of the lost son except the lost one who has received the warm and repeated kisses of the Father and felt the beating of His loving, compassionate heart. These truths must be experienced, not merely studied. This does not mean that we must go into sin as the lost son did. But we have all gone into the distant country.

The word *prodigal,* which is often used to refer to this son, does not refer to his sin of lust but to his free and reckless use of the money his father had given him. We have all been prodigals with the Father's gifts. All we have, we have received of Him; yet we have lived as though Christ had never died. We have lived with self at the center, away from the compassionate, loving heart and home of the Father.

When we come to ourselves, we hope to receive the place of a hired servant, though we do not deserve even that. It never enters our mind to imagine the love and mercy of a God who can forgive and treat us as though we had never sinned. Do we know this in our hearts? Or have we done as thousands of church members in Christian homes have done—namely, taken all this marvelous love for granted?

The reason many know little of the wonder of forgiving grace is that they have known little of a powerful conviction of sin. They have been Pharisees rather than repentant tax collectors. If we have not committed sins of the flesh, let us praise the Lord for His restraining grace. But let us also enter into the depth of shame and poverty of the lost son, the realization that we are "dead" and "lost," in order that the wonder of the heavenly Father's heart may break upon us in all its glory.

And have we learned the lesson of the Father's heart toward the child who is staying at home? After that first great rejoicing of the Father at my repentance, does His interest in me wane? Am I an older brother dwelling in the Father's house but without the joy and riches that belong to me as His son?

The Father's heart is expressed in compassion toward the lost and in forgiveness and restoration toward the penitent, but that same heart of love is expressed toward His child by giving him all that He has: "For if, when we were God's enemies, we were reconciled to him through the death of his son, how much more, having been reconciled, shall we be saved through his life" (Rom. 5:10). Let us then enjoy the Father's bounty, "his glorious riches in Christ Jesus" (Phil. 4:19), the peace that passes understanding, the fullness of His Spirit, the joy unspeakable and full of glory.

Finally, let us share the joy of the Father in welcoming the returning prodigal—indeed, making the whole of our life and service to center in bringing home lost souls and thus sharing the Father's own joy.

REVIEW OF LESSON 4

1. What do you think of the interpretation that the lost son represents a Christian who has gone astray and that the teaching is that a straying Christian will always return?

2. Did our Lord want to affect the lives of both tax collectors and Pharisees with this parable? How are each represented in the parable?

3. Can the younger son represent the Gentiles and the older brother the Jews? In what way? Do they also represent us?

4. In what way is this a deeper revelation of the Father's heart than what is given in the parables of the lost sheep and the lost coin?

5. What does the story of the older brother reveal concerning the Father's heart, and how does this apply to us?

PART III

PARABLES
OF THE
CHRISTIAN'S HEART

PREPARATION FOR LESSON 5

Reading Lesson: Luke 18:9-14; 7:36-50

1. What, do you think, would the people who first heard this parable think of bringing together a Pharisee and a tax collector in the same story?

2. How does the character of the Pharisee who went into the temple to pray compare with that of Simon, the Pharisee to whom Jesus told the parable of the two debtors?

3. What is the central message of the parable of the two debtors? How is this truth illustrated by Simon the Pharisee and by the sinful woman who anointed the Lord?

4. What are the good points and bad points of the Pharisee as revealed in the parable of the Pharisee and the tax collector?

5. Was the sinful woman forgiven because of her love for Jesus? What was the basis of her forgiveness?

Lesson 5

The Pharisee and the Tax Collector
The Two Debtors

Luke 18:10-14; Luke 7:41-42

The foundation of all truth is God Himself. The first question to be answered is, Who is God? What kind of a being is He? The parables of the Father's heart have answered that question. He is a Father, and He is love. He is holy and cannot fellowship with sin. He is the heavenly Father, the Infinite One, the Creator, and the Judge. The parables reveal His heart and show that at the center of His holiness and His infinite perfection is His love.

Following this discovery of the heart of God is the question as to what the heart of man should be in his relation to God and to his fellow men. There are five parables of our Lord that answer this question in a most remarkable and searching way.

THE PHARISEE AND THE TAX COLLECTOR

The Setting (Luke 18:9)

The story of the two men, a Pharisee and a tax collector, who went up into the temple to pray, is often classed as a prayer parable. It does contain a lesson on the right attitude in prayer. But is that the essential or central truth of the parable? There are a number of rich messages and spiritual lessons in every parable, but all of these center in one great truth. The setting frequently gives the key to this truth. How is the setting presented in this parable?

Note that there is no direct connection with what has gone before except that Jesus has just told the parable of the widow and the unjust judge. Since Luke tells that He spoke the parable to "some who were confident of their own righteousness and looked down on everybody else," we know that the central thought is not the prayer and the way to pray but the matter of self-righteousness.

Here again a full understanding of the setting requires a knowledge of the people of our Lord's day. The story shows that the Pharisees were the special representatives of this spirit, and our Lord's experiences with them become part of the setting of the parable.

The Story (Luke 18:10-14)

In this story we notice again that our Lord's illustrations were startling. To us the parable of the Pharisee and the tax collector means what this and other parables have made them mean. But to those who heard the story for the first time it was a bold and daring thing for a teacher to bring together a Pharisee, a member of the orthodox party and of high social standing, and a tax collector, a symbol of rejection and hatred—making the tax collector the one whom God accepts and the Pharisee the one whom God rejects. Thus again we have illustrated the importance of learning the historical background through the study of both the setting and the story itself.

Write down several characteristics of this story, as a story. Have you noted any special difference between this story and the stories of the sower and the four kinds of soil? Some parable stories have no special teaching in themselves; but here we have an account of two men, with two different attitudes in their prayer, and the story itself has in it a spiritual message.

Nevertheless, it is important to distinguish between the story and the spiritual message. For the truth is far wider and deeper than its application to these two men and their prayer. Men today do not go into the temple to pray as they did, and the self-righteous man of today would not express this self-righteousness in the way this Pharisee did. So we must study the story itself and then seek to find the great spiritual message. A good way to do this is to sketch the characters of the two men as revealed in the story.

This Pharisee was a religious man. He was a praying man. He was a regular worshiper of God. He was orthodox. He was an honest man. He was just. He was a zealous seeker after God, to the extent of fasting twice a week. He was a scrupulous tither. We are taking his own confession concerning himself as true, for the point of this parable is not the hypocrisy of the man. With all these good things to his account, what was wrong with him? His heart toward God was absolutely wrong.

An important element in the teaching here, as nearly always in the parables, is contrast. The tax collector has an attitude in prayer that is right toward God. In a few words we get a picture of a humble, broken, and contrite spirit who counted himself utterly unworthy to come into the presence of a holy God, deeply sorry for his sin, and with no thought of the sins or faults of others, and casting himself on the mercy of God.

The Spiritual Message (Luke 18:14)

Notice how closely in this parable the message is linked with the story itself. For the story is spiritual. "I tell you that this man, rather than the other, went home justified before God." These words of our Lord may be taken as part of the story itself or as the spiritual message. What is the central message? Shall we say it is a lesson in humility, as suggested by the words of our Lord, "For everyone who exalts himself will be humbled, and he who humbles himself will be exalted"? It *is* a lesson on humility, but here we have a particular application of humility.

The parable gives a picture of what the sinner's attitude should be toward the holy, merciful, and compassionate God. The Pharisee is a picture of how not to come to God. The Pharisee justified himself. God condemned him. The Pharisee said, "I am all right." God said, "You are all wrong." The tax collector condemned himself. God justified him. The tax collector said, "I am all wrong." God said, "You are now right in my sight."

The expression that the tax collector was justified "rather than the other" does not mean that there was a relative difference between them. The Pharisee was not justified at all, but condemned. The relative expression is often found in Scripture as a figure of speech for the absolute. But in this case the more accurate rendering of the words translated "rather than" would be "contrary to." He was justified and *not* the other.

Here, then, is the first teaching on what the heart of the Christian should be. In order to become a Christian, a man must come as a broken-hearted sinner, with a humble and contrite heart, casting himself on the mercy of God. Every man must begin there. Every man must continue there, with this attitude toward God. Before God I have no righteousness of my own; so all boasting or trust in myself and my works must be excluded, and I must in humility cast myself on the mercy of God. This is the message of Romans 3:26-27. Faith excludes boasting.

Does this parable teach the Atonement through the blood of Christ? As in many other teachings in the Gospels, the death of Christ is the vital center—even though it is not directly in view. Direct and full teaching is not given on the meaning of the Cross until after the death and resurrection of our Lord.

Some commentators have held that the concept of propitiation for sin is contained in the prayer of the tax collector. It is doubtful that our Lord intended to suggest that this man understood the meaning of propitiation for sin. He cried for mercy. Yet the very word *mercy* shows that forgiveness is possible with God only because there has been a propitiation provided. A man with the humble heart of the tax collector would be eager to accept the blood of Christ shed for his sins. Thus he would have the joy of forgiveness and justification. The tax collector of the parable is one who not only asks for mercy but also receives and rejoices in peace with God.

The Personal Application

It may be thought scarcely necessary to add any suggestion on the personal application of a parable so plain in its meaning. But perhaps we should stop to ask ourselves, How readily can I identify myself as either a Pharisee or a tax collector?

This parable suggests that all men are divided into these two classes. With respect to the attitude of our heart toward God, we are either a Pharisee or a tax collector. Which are we by nature? What was the sin of the Pharisee? He justified himself. Is that something I have ever done? Is it something I can very easily do? Then by nature I have the heart of a Pharisee. The Pharisee condemned others. Is it easier for me to see the faults in others than to observe my own? Then I have the heart of a Pharisee.

Turning to the positive side, let us each ask: Have I ever taken the place of the tax collector who saw himself a lost sinner, deserving only God's condemnation and having hope only in His mercy? Have I called myself "a sinner," as the tax collector did, the sinner for whom Christ died because of the mercy of God?

If not, then I have not made the beginning of having the right heart attitude toward God. The reason many are not sure of their salvation is that they have never been sure of their damnation, that is, sure that this is what they deserved. To know the joy of being saved, I must know that I was a lost sinner.

Christians are too apt to take this for granted; that is, rather than facing the *fact* that we are sinners, we merely accept the *theory*. The tax collector was repenting of his sin. There is too much attempted "belief" in Christ without the repentance that makes the belief real.

It is true that we must only believe, but saving faith includes real repentance. That is why the gospel message is a message to repent and believe. *Repentance* and faith and remission of sins is to be preached in His name to all nations (Luke 24:47). Paul's commission was to preach to the Gentiles that they should repent and do works worthy of repentance, that is, to prove it was genuine (Acts 26:20).

As this attitude of heart is the one key to enter the door of peace with God, so it is the secret of continuing with the right attitude each time we pray, that is, the attitude of a humble and contrite heart. We can come now with the joy of being accepted in the Beloved, as one who has obtained the mercy of God yet always recognizing that it is mercy that we need as we bow before His throne of grace.

The Two Debtors

The Setting (Luke 7:36-40)

This parable is a very brief and simple one: "Two men owed money to a certain moneylender. One owed him five hundred denarii, and the other fifty. Neither of them had the money to pay him back, so he canceled the debts of both. Now which of them will love him more?" (Luke 7:41-42). But in the case of this parable, the setting is really a vital part of the story and presents one of the most touching and dramatic scenes of the Gospels. It was, indeed, as are many of the miracles and scenes in the Gospels, an acted-out parable.

Simon the Pharisee (spiritual kin of the Pharisee who went to the temple to pray) invited our Lord to have dinner with him. At this point we need to know something of the customs of that day in order to picture the scene that followed. In a house such as Simon's there was an open court into which strangers or the poor could come and watch the diners. The guests reclined on couches, with their feet extended away from the table. Thus it would be natural for the woman to stand at the feet of Jesus. The guests, as they came in, would first be given water and the servants would bathe their feet after their sandals were removed. The host would greet the guest with a kiss of welcome and would anoint his head with oil. These were standard courtesies.

It seems inconceivable that Simon should point our Lord to a seat, or allow Him to find a seat, and not show Him any of the courtesies due an honored guest. Had he known he was entertaining the Lord of glory, the King of Israel, Jehovah his God, how differently he would have acted! Yet his heart would not have been different. And because he did not extend these courtesies, we have opportunity to see what was really in his heart.

The sinful woman comes with her alabaster jar of perfume and her broken, contrite heart, and she weeps as she anoints her Savior and Lord, oblivious of Simon and all the other guests. This Jesus, Simon thinks, were He a prophet, would have known what sort of woman this is, a sinful woman, morally impure.

Here we have a glimpse of why Simon invited the Lord. He wanted to have a close view of this Rabbi to determine if He was really a prophet. He was a judge of the One before whom he should have humbly knelt to have his own heart judged. He himself was judged in the white light of that loving Judge and Discerner of the thoughts of the heart. Simon thinks that the Lord does not know this woman's heart. But it is Simon who does not know.

Christ knows the woman's heart, and also Simon's. Here again we have two hearts pictured, and each of us has either the heart of Simon or the heart of that woman.

The Story (Luke 7:41-42)

The Lord Jesus, looking into the heart of Simon ("He knew what was in a man" [John 2:25]), told him the simple parable of the two debtors. This story seems almost incidental to the drama that preceded it and the application that follows. But it is important to note the one central theme of the story. The question is not how the two men got into debt, or on what ground they were forgiven. The whole emphasis is on the fact that the lender forgave them both, and the point of the story is found in the question our Lord asked Simon, "Which of them will love him more?"

We have noted that a characteristic of the parables is that they compel moral assent; the listener must always accept the lesson intended by our Lord. So Simon grudgingly admits, "I suppose the one who had the bigger debt canceled." The amount of the debt is not the issue here. The sole point intended is the principle that the measure of love is the measure of the gift that has been received.

The Spiritual Message (Luke 7:44-50)

"Do you see this woman?" our Lord asks Simon. He asks this question of all who read the parable. What a stinging but loving rebuke Simon now receives as our Lord draws the contrast between the heart of Simon and the heart of the woman.

The woman becomes a mirror in which he may see himself. He gave no water. She has not ceased to wet her Lord's feet with the sweet water of a repentant heart. Simon gave Jesus no kiss, but she had "not stopped kissing" His feet. The word for an overflowing affection is used (the same intensive word used when Judas kissed his Master to betray Him). Simon did not anoint the head of his honored Guest, but she gave possibly all her wealth to anoint His feet.

What is the central truth of the parable and of the actual scene that is so much more tremendous than the simple parable? "Therefore, I tell you, her many sins have been forgiven—for she loved much. But he who has been forgiven little loves little."

These words have been taken to mean that she was forgiven as a reward for her love. But the whole point of the teaching is that she loved as a result of the great forgiveness, not that the forgiveness was the result of the love. Our Lord's parting words to her showed the condition of her forgiveness, "Your faith has saved you; go in peace."

Here, then, is the second lesson concerning the Christian's heart. After one has come as the tax collector, and as this sinful woman, and has received the word of forgiveness and peace, the heart goes out in great love toward the Savior who has loved and saved.

Christ has forgiven me, the chief of sinners, my great mountain of sin because of His compassionate love for me. Recognizing this, my heart is filled with devoted, passionate love for Him. This love does not save me, but it is the fruit of my salvation. Simon the Pharisee loved little. This is a figure of speech. He loved not at all. He did not acknowledge that he had any sins to be forgiven.

The Personal Application

To study and to understand the message of this parable is to make the personal application. Yet it may be well to ask ourselves again if we have the heart of this woman. We might argue that we have not sinned as this woman has. If we have really learned the message of the first parable and have taken the place of the penitent tax collector, then we are ready to understand the heart of this woman and to realize that of us also it can be said, his "many sins."

This parable and its setting bring to light two revelations of God's Word that the human heart is slow to accept. The first concerns the awfulness of sin. This woman realized it. Simon did not. Have we acknowledged God's estimate of our own heart, that it is deceitful above all things and desperately wicked?

Secondly, this parable reveals the wonders of redeeming love. A sinner like the woman in this story can be washed white as snow. She knew it and was overwhelmed with gratitude for the One who had worked this miracle. Simon did not believe it. He thought he knew the woman's condition as hopeless and his own heart as needing little change. But he knew neither the blackness of his own heart nor the whiteness of the heart cleansed through faith.

Realizing these two wonders, the wonder of His matchless grace and our own unworthiness, is to enter into the message of this parable and to learn the second secret of what God wants the Christian's heart to be.

REVIEW OF LESSON 5

1. In what ways may a Christian today have the heart of the Pharisee?

2. What is the central message of the parable of the two debtors?

3. What does the parable of the Pharisee and the tax collector teach concerning how we are saved?

4. What does the parable of the Pharisee and the tax collector teach about repentance? Is it possible to believe in Christ and be saved without repenting?

5. What does the incident of Simon and the sinful woman reveal about the character of Jesus? What does it show about the way He was regarded by others?

PREPARATION FOR LESSON 6

Reading Lesson: Matthew 18:1-35; Luke 14:1-11; 10:25-37

1. What is the "immediate" setting of the parable of the unmerciful servant?

2. Does this story seem to be true to life? Can you think of times in which we display a spirit such as this servant had?

3. What was Peter's idea of forgiving those who sinned against him? Was he right or wrong?

4. What is the central message of the parable of the lowest seat at the feast?

5. How does this apply to our lives?

Lesson 6

The Unmerciful Servant
The Lowest Seat at the Feast
The Good Samaritan

Matthew 18:23-34; Luke 14:8-10; Luke 10:30-35

We have learned in the two parables studied in the last lesson that men should first have a humble and contrite heart in coming to God for mercy, then a heart of loving gratitude toward God our Savior who in His great love has forgiven and restored. The next question follows, What should the attitude of the Christian be toward the man who has sinned against him?

The answer is given in an unforgettable way in the parable of the unmerciful servant.

THE UNMERCIFUL SERVANT

The Setting (Matt. 18:15-22)

The parable of the unmerciful servant is found in Matthew 18. What other parable does this chapter contain? What seems to be the teaching of the chapter as a whole? Read Matthew 16:21 and notice that a new stage in the ministry of Christ begins here, as He seeks to tell His disciples of His approach-

73

ing death on the cross. From this time on, the teaching is especially for the inner circle of disciples.

In this chapter, for example, He is instructing them on the meaning of true greatness and the relationship of believers to one another. In other words, He is seeking to have them understand the spirit of the Cross, the meaning of taking up the Cross and following Him (Matt. 16:24).

After teaching them about becoming as little children and having the attitude toward children and childlike believers that the heavenly Father has (18:1-14), He takes up the question of forgiving a brother who sins against them. Then follows the marvelous statement about two persons asking about the same thing and the explanation that it shall be given them: "For where two or three come together in my name, there am I with them" (v. 20). This is a wonderful revelation concerning the relation of Christians—they are joined with Christ, and He is in their midst.

Peter passes over this wonderful revelation and goes back to the question of forgiving his brother. Peter sees a problem. "Lord, how many times shall I forgive my brother when he sins against me?" is Peter's question.

This question we may call the *immediate* setting of the parable of the unmerciful servant. For it is in answer to that question that our Lord gives the parable. Or rather it is in illustrating His own answer that He gives the parable.

We have seen that a full study of the setting includes not only this immediate context but the remote context. In this case we first study the whole chapter and then go on to study the relation of this chapter to the whole of Matthew. In many cases it is important in the full understanding of a parable to notice what place it has in the ministry and teaching of Christ, namely the place it has in relation to the whole Gospel in which it occurs.

Now notice that Peter does not merely ask how often he

should forgive his sinning brother. He gives a suggestion of his own—"Up to seven times?" What was in Peter's mind when he made this suggestion? Is it a generous suggestion, a willingness to forgive an erring brother seven times? Those of us who can recall an injury done to us, an injury that we by the grace of the Lord have freely forgiven and then have had that wrong repeated a second and a third time, can perhaps sympathize with Peter. Is there not to be a limit to human kindness and endurance? But suppose our Lord forgave us seven times and then ceased? Note the answer of Christ to Peter's question: "I tell you, not seven times, but seventy-seven times."

How much of a mistake had Peter made? It was not a mistake in mathematics. Did our Lord mean literally to forgive seventy-seven times and then stop? Again where would we be if our Lord stopped at that number? Seven is often called the perfect number. Seventy-seven is a figure of speech for an unlimited number, the real perfection of forgiveness that is not governed by number but by something else. Then follows the parable with its searching teaching.

What has the setting prepared us to expect as the one central message of this parable? It is a teaching on the attitude the Christian should have toward those who sin against him.

Before leaving the setting, we may notice that the teaching about forgiveness here has primarily to do with the relation of fellow Christians, members of the church, His body, which our Lord has been telling them is to be built. He has given instruction as to how to treat a brother who sins and will not repent. Such a person is to be regarded as the Gentile and the tax collector.

That does not mean we are to cease to love him, for we are to love the Gentile and the tax collector and seek to win them to Christ. But it means they are to be regarded as having put themselves outside the circle of Christian friends. But it will be seen that the teaching of the parable goes deeper than the application to Christian brethren and has to do with our attitude toward all men.

The Story (Matt. 18:23-34)

The greatest blessing will be received from studying the parables if we study the Bible text for ourselves before studying the suggestions of a human teacher. Therefore, if you have not already done so, stop here and study this story as a story, answering the following questions:

What facts about the historical background do I need to understand to make the story clear to me? The historical background means the customs of the time as shown in the story, especially those customs or ways of speaking and acting that are different from our own.

Is this story true to life or are there some features that seem not to be true to life?

Name several striking characteristics of the story, as a story—its length, its human interest, its quality of compelling moral assent, its vivid details.

Compare this story with other parables we have studied and note any differences.

What is the one central theme of the story? How do the various characters and the various details of the story all climax in this central theme?

An important part of this story is the debt of ten thousand talents as contrasted with the debt of one hundred denarii. These amounts have to be translated into the economy of more modern times in order to appreciate the effect the story would have on those who first heard it. The denarius was a day's wage in those times. The talent was worth about thirty-three hundred denarii. In modern times, if we consider a day's wage to be twenty-five dollars, the one hundred denarii would be worth twenty-five hundred dollars and the ten thousand talents would be worth $825 million. That is quite a contrast!

The historical background also suggests the customs of those days in regard to the incurring of debt, the selling into slavery, the casting into prison, and the delivering to the jailers. Are these details true to life? Again, are the contracting of such an enormous debt and its free forgiveness true to life? We need to understand the despotic kings of that time, acting as it pleased them, but in any case the story is undoubtedly an unusual one.

When we say the parable is true to life, it does not mean that it is necessarily what happens in real life. The parable contains what may be *possible* in real experience, and frequently a story is heightened in order to illustrate more accurately the spiritual lesson. Other parables, of course, give incidents that are common in everyday experience. Another interesting difference of this parable is that the message is given through the picture of the negative side, the unforgiving spirit.

The human interest of this story is very marked, and we can judge that the attitude of the listeners toward the unmerciful servant of the parable would be one of violent condemnation.

The chief need in understanding the story itself is to appreciate its central theme. The many vivid details of this story—the enormous debt, the decision to sell the debtor and his family, the plea for mercy, the unexpected compassion and free forgiveness of the debt—all of these interesting facts are preparatory to something else. The servant goes out and finds a fellow servant who owes him a relatively small sum. How will this debt now appear to the man who has just been released from what must have been a crushing burden as he awaited the inevitable accounting on the part of the king?

Does he, with a heart overflowing with joy in his new-found

freedom, tell his fellow servant that he has forgotten all about that little debt? Does he gladly cancel it? No, this is not the way the story reads. It is hard to believe that he should take him by the throat and demand the payment and then, refusing his plea for patience, put him into prison. Is this part of the story true to life? There follows the revealing of the facts to the lord by the other servants who are grieved at such conduct; then comes the wrath of the lord and the reversal of the former forgiveness; the judgment falls, and the unmerciful servant must repay the entire debt, even as he asked his fellow servant to do.

The Spiritual Message (Matt. 18:35)

We have suggested that it was almost unthinkable that a servant should act in the way the unmerciful servant did. But the sad truth is that it gives a real picture of the way the natural human heart treats those who offend us. What is the central spiritual teaching of the parable? It is given in words that sound strange indeed from the lips of the compassionate and tender Savior, speaking of His heavenly Father: "This is how my heavenly Father will treat each of you unless you forgive your brother from your heart."

What does it mean that Christians will be brought before the magistrates? What does this parable teach regarding the disciples and their relation to the Lord? Will Peter and the others ever sin in this way and lose their salvation?

Let us not make the mistake of seeking an answer to these questions in the parable. Let us ask the parable only one question. What is the great central message we are to gather from this parable? Is it not a message concerning the Christian's attitude toward those who have sinned against him? And once more, this attitude must be the result of what God's heart toward us has been.

So let us state the teaching thus: As God has forgiven me a

debt of sin against Him that is beyond all reckoning, I must from my heart forgive my brother who has sinned against me. These wrongs are as nothing compared with what I have been forgiven. I do not forgive men in order to be forgiven but because I have been forgiven.

This truth has an application both to professing Christians who are not saved and to real Christians. One who persists in his unforgiving spirit may by that indicate that he has never been born of the Spirit. A true Christian who holds an unforgiving spirit will be chastened by the Lord, even to the extent of losing his physical life (cf. 1 Cor. 11:30-32). The withdrawal of the remission of the debt by the king in the parable does not mean that the Lord withdraws his salvation from the saved man, or that He has ever granted His salvation to the professing Christian who is not saved. The parable teaching is a warning to all professing Christians; the real Christian evidences the fact that he is saved by heeding the warning.

Frequently the question is raised as to whether we should forgive sins that are not repented of. This parable applies primarily to sins that are repented of. As our Lord says in another teaching on this same subject, "If [your brother] sins against you seven times in a day, and seven times comes back to you and says, 'I repent,' forgive him" (Luke 17:4).

But this does not mean that we can hold an unforgiving spirit until our brother does repent. It is our forgiving spirit before he repents that makes possible full and free forgiveness when he does repent.

The Personal Application

Just because the action of this unmerciful servant is so contrary to our sense of justice, we may too easily conclude that we ourselves would never be guilty of such a spirit. But let us ask if we really have the Spirit of the Lord Jesus or the spirit of this servant toward those who sin against us. Do the sins of others against us really appear as little in contrast with the much that we owe our Lord? Is not the thought of our natural heart rather to minimize our own sins against God and magnify the seriousness of the sins of others against us? These parables are searching indeed.

A practical application of the truth of this parable is constantly before us in the petition in the Lord's Prayer, "Forgive us our debts, as we also have forgiven our debtors" (Matt. 6:12). How striking it is that after He has finished praying our Lord refers back to this petition and says, "For if you forgive men when they sin against you, your heavenly Father will also forgive you. But if you do not forgive men their sins, your Father will not forgive your sins" (vv. 14-15).

Again in Mark 11:22-26, in that marvelous promise concerning prayer and its answer, our Lord adds the solemn warning that when we stand praying we should forgive others for whatever they may have done to us, that the heavenly Father may forgive us. For an unforgiven intercessor is an unanswered intercessor. How vital and central is this matter of forgiveness.

At the close of a Bible conference, a young woman was conversing with the speaker.

"Sir," she said, "the girl who gave her testimony today talked about a friend who had not spoken to her for six weeks. Well, I'm that friend."

"Have you decided now to go and make up with her?" asked the Bible teacher.

"I have surrendered everything else in my life to the Lord except that," she protested.

"I think we should talk more about this," he said, "but first let's pray. Would you begin?"

They sat down. Finally, after a few moments of silence, he whispered, "Pray the Lord's Prayer."

Soon the young woman began to pray, though in a rather

petulant tone: "Our Father, who art in heaven, hallowed be thy name. Thy kingdom come. Thy will be done, on earth as it is in heaven. Give us this day our daily bread . . ."

There was silence once again.

"What's wrong?" he asked.

But there was no answer.

Finally, he asked, "How have you been praying for the last six weeks?"

"I haven't been praying," she answered.

This is a vivid illustration of the truth that no one who deliberately refuses to forgive another can pray effectively. He or she can only "say prayers."

But no one who holds an unforgiving spirit, even if they are doing so unintentionally, can be assured of answers to prayer. This young woman did surrender her life and ask forgiveness for her sin and, needless to say, the first thing she planned to do was to go to her friend and ask forgiveness, having first forgiven her from her heart.

When the love of God is shed abroad in our hearts by the Holy Spirit, that love goes out in forgiving grace toward every one of our debtors in the same way that God's love freely forgave us of our great mountain of sin.

THE LOWEST SEAT AT THE FEAST

We have studied the attitude of the heart, first as a sinner before the holy but merciful God, and second as a forgiven and cleansed sinner toward Christ, and third as a forgiven sinner in relation to a brother who has sinned. Now we ask the question, What should be the attitude of the Christian's heart toward others in the social realm? The answer is given in the parable of the lowest seat at the feast.

The Setting (Luke 14:7)

Again we find our Lord dining in the house of a ruler of the Pharisees on the Sabbath day. Just before the parable in Luke 14:3, we read our Lord's question to the lawyers and Pharisees as to whether it is lawful to heal on the Sabbath, because a man with dropsy had come before Him. There was no answer; and Jesus healed the man, sent him out, and then spoke the brief parable of the donkey or ox fallen into a pit on the Sabbath day. This incident shows the great difference there was between the spirit of the Lord and the spirit of these Pharisees, and this was evident throughout His ministry.

The immediate occasion of the parable is given in verse 7: "When he noticed how the guests picked the places of honor at the table, he told them this parable." We have classed this as a parable on the Christian's heart attitude, and again we notice that the heart attitude of the Pharisees is set in contrast to that of Christ.

The Story (Luke 14:8-10)

This parable, the story itself, is really a direct bit of counsel as to what the hearer's action should be when invited to a marriage feast. We have already seen that the word *parable* is used in a very free way to apply to any kind of comparison or illustration. But this is a true parable, even though the guests whom our Lord is addressing are used as the actors in the story. A study of the customs of the times shows that this story is true to life. Seating guests according to their social standing also became traditional in Middle Eastern countries. The same principle can be seen in Western lands, though not carried out in such direct and naive ways.

Notice that our Lord does not here condemn this practice. He is merely stating the fact and recalling what doubtless happened more than once: a guest taking his place, reclining on the couch, and then having to go to the lowest place because a more honorable guest came late and all the intermediate places were filled. Our Lord recognizes that some men may be more honorable than others and, in spite of all the false distinctions made by men, there are certain true distinctions, in the very nature of things, that must be recognized.

If the parable were in the form of other parables, the story would go on to tell of a man who took the lowest seat and then had the honor of going higher. But in this case our Lord gives the direct advice that they should take the lowest place. But notice that this advice or teaching concerns the outward act at a feast rather than the spiritual message that is hidden in the parable.

The Spiritual Message (Luke 14:11)

"For everyone who exalts himself will be humbled, and he who humbles himself will be exalted." Our Lord thus gives the spiritual message of this parable in the same words as those He uses in the parable of the Pharisee and the tax collector in Luke 18:14. In each case the central message is humility. But the message has a different application in the two parables. What is the one central teaching in this parable?

"Whenever I want to be exalted, I just humble myself," a Christian said to a minister friend, apparently in all seriousness. This may be taken as an amusing illustration of a wrong interpretation of the parable. It also helps to emphasize the *true* teaching of the right heart attitude, of which this conduct at a marriage feast would be just one illustration. The Christian is one who in all relationships of life puts others before himself.

The Holy Spirit gives this same teaching through Paul in Philippians: "In humility consider others better than yourselves" (2:3). In that chapter the Lord Jesus Himself is held up as the great example of humility. He was the one who came from the heights of glory to the depths of humiliation and shame. "Your attitude should be the same as that of Christ Jesus" (v. 5). The heart of the Christian is to be a heart like Christ's in this respect as in all others.

If the ruler of the Pharisees at this feast was like Simon the Pharisee, mentioned in Luke 7, he left our Lord to find His own seat. We can well believe, then, that the parable was spoken from the lowest seat at that feast. The Lord of glory humbled Himself, as so wonderfully described in Philippians 2, and He was exalted to the heights of glory, as shown in the same chapter. Yet we can readily see that He did not humble Himself in order that He could be exalted. The Lord Jesus was humility incarnate.

In the same way the Christian is to humble himself, counting each other better than himself when it comes to a matter of precedence. This does not mean that we are to consider that others necessarily can do certain work more skillfully than ourselves. It is the heart attitude of humility that takes the lowest place in all contacts with our fellow men. It is a searching test of character.

The Good Samaritan

We have listed the good Samaritan as the fifth parable in the series on the Christian's heart. This parable has already been fully treated in the second lesson, where we used it to illustrate the principles to be used in interpreting parables. Here we will notice briefly its relation to these other four parables.

There is a definite progression of teaching concerning the right heart attitude in these four parables we have just studied: first, the sinner comes with a humble, contrite heart, casting himself on the mercy of God; second, he is forgiven and his heart is filled with overflowing gratitude and love toward the Savior; third, he in turn has the same heart of forgiving love toward his fellows who have sinned against him, recognizing that their sin against him is as nothing compared with what God has forgiven in him; and fourth, his heart attitude is also affected in all his social relations with others, apart from the question of their sin against him.

A further step is taken in the parable of the good Samaritan. We have seen its teaching to be that the Christian is a neighbor and is to be instant in season and out to serve unselfishly those in need. This is a heart attitude toward others and is another outworking of the change that comes when the penitent sinner is saved.

As we look back over the parables, we notice how impossible it is for the natural man to take the attitude that the parables require. The natural man acts in just the opposite way from these teachings. He does not prefer others before himself nor live for the sake of unselfish service.

Here we find the answer to the question raised in lesson 2 concerning the relation of good deeds to our salvation. The lawyer had asked Christ what he must do to inherit eternal life, and we noted that some claim that Christ told the lawyer to go and do these kind deeds and he would be saved. The truth is that this lawyer needed a change of heart before he would or could do those deeds.

The parable of the good Samaritan should have brought him to the conviction of sin and the need of a Savior. When we accept Christ, the love of God is shed abroad in our hearts through the Holy Spirit whom He gives to us (Rom. 5:5). Christ living in me is the only secret for my living as Christ lived (Gal. 2:20).

If we are saved, does this mean that we instinctively act as Christ acted and that we carry out perfectly all these attitudes of heart? If we were at once made perfectly like Christ, this might be the result. In that case we would not need to study the parables.

Yet it is through the truth that we are sanctified. And there is a human side to it. We on our part are to study the Word and test our lives by it. When we are convicted of having fallen short, we do not strive in human power to carry out our Lord's teachings. That would be to live according to the law. But we recognize that only through His divine power may we have this attitude that will lead us in fuller and fuller measure to act at all times like the good Samaritan and like the other examples of the parables. In a word, we shall be made more and more like Christ Himself.

Our blessed Lord is the revelation of what the Father's heart is. He also is Himself the revelation of what the Father would have the heart of His children to be—apart from that great exception that He had no sin and needed no change.

The measure in which we have learned these parables, therefore, is the measure of our likeness to Christ. Have we learned the parables? Each will confess that we have not learned them perfectly. But now, at this moment, we may enter into the miracle experience of a heart like Christ. How? By faith. As the lost sinner repents and accepts the free gift of life by faith, so the defeated Christian may confess, yield his life anew to Christ, and trust Him who saved him to keep him.

"So then just as you received Christ Jesus our Lord, continue to live in Him" (Col. 2:6). If you are saved by faith you are to live by faith. Faith says, "Christ lives in me." Do you believe it?

REVIEW OF LESSON 6

1. How does the parable of the unmerciful servant help us to understand what the Lord's Prayer says about forgiveness?

2. What might the parable of the lowest seat have to say about how we are to assess our own abilities?

3. Give an illustration from your own experience or from the experience of others of the spirit shown by the unmerciful servant and by those who chose the chief seats. Are these common attitudes?

4. How was the lawyer's question about inheriting eternal life answered by the parable of the good Samaritan?

5. What does the parable of the good Samaritan have to do with salvation? How are kind deeds related to salvation?

PART IV

PARABLES
OF
SERVICE

PREPARATION FOR LESSON 7

Reading Lesson: Luke 17:1-10

1. Why did the disciples say to the Lord: "Increase our faith" (v. 5)?
2. Relate this request to verses 1-4.
3. Why, do you think, did Christ tell this parable?
4. This parable has been called the parable of "extra service." Was the servant in this story doing extra service?
5. Tell in your own words the central truth of the parable.

Lesson 7

The Unworthy Servant

Luke 17:7-9

The parable of the unworthy servant has been considered a puzzling and difficult passage by many. Few Christians, apparently, have received any spiritual blessing from it. The Bible warns against being unworthy servants: for example, in the parable of the talents, the unworthy servant is cast into outer darkness. But here the disciples are told to call themselves unworthy servants. The word "unworthy" has a different significance here.

So the question remains, What does the parable mean? There is a rich spiritual message in it concerning service, and we have placed it first among parables of service because it gives a foundation secret for the right attitude in Christian living and service.

The Setting (Luke 17:1-6)

This is one of twenty parables recorded by Luke in the famous Perean section of his Gospel—9:51 to 19:28. In this section our Lord is journeying toward Jerusalem and the Cross. Of these twenty, fifteen are found in Luke only, including this story of the unworthy servant. It is closely related to the parables in chapters 15 and 16; apparently it was on that same occasion when the tax collectors and sinners were present and the scribes and Pharisees murmured against Him that our Lord gave this additional teaching to the disciples.

First, He warns them against being occasions of stumbling (Luke 17:1-2). This has direct reference to the Pharisees, who were putting stumbling blocks in the way of the tax collectors and sinners who were coming to the Savior (15:1-2; 16:14-17). The disciples were not guilty of this, but they were to take heed lest they have an unforgiving spirit. While they were not to be occasions of stumbling to others, they were to be ready to forgive those who did offend against them and then repented. A forgiving spirit is to be present even toward those who do not repent, but there is a sense in which one cannot be forgiven until he repents, and it is in this sense the word is used here.

It was evidently in response to these teachings that the apostles said to the Lord, "Increase our faith." If they were to reach such standards of Christian conduct, they felt the need of added grace. His answer gives them a startling view of faith: it is not the bigness of faith, but the greatness of the miracle-working God in whom the faith rests. Faith like a tiny grain of mustard seed (a well-known symbol for minuteness), if really used, could work a miracle such as rooting up the tree that was near them and planting it in the sea.

There is an indirect suggestion here that the disciples were asking Him to increase something they really did not have. They needed to see what faith really meant, as they did after His death and resurrection and the descent of the Holy Spirit. They did, indeed, have some faith, and our Lord was seeking to strengthen it by showing them what faith really meant.

If a man should have such faith so as to root up trees or remove mountains and should keep the commands of the Lord about causing none to stumble and about forgiving the brother who sins against us, he might be puffed up and decide that he had attained a high place as a servant of Christ. High Christian attainment and notable success in Christian service foster pride unless the heart is guarded against it. Our Lord, therefore, adds a parable to give the disciples the right view of their relation to Him and to His commands. A heart of true humility in living and service will result from entering, by His grace, into the secret of this parable. First, let us study the story.

The Story (Luke 17:7-9)

A noted scholar has called this the parable of extra service, suggesting that just as the servant came from the field weary from his day's toil and had additional work given him in preparing his master's meal, so a Christian may be called on for extra service and should be ready to do it with a glad and willing spirit. It is true that Christians are called upon for "extra" service of all kinds, even beyond what might reasonably be expected of them, but a study of this story indicates that its central point is that no extra service has been done.

The "servant" in this story is a bondslave, belonging to his master. He is not working a predetermined number of hours each day. Nor is he a farmhand employed to plow fields or care for sheep while the cook takes care of the meals. He is a slave who does what his master tells him to do.

Our Lord is not dealing with the question of whether it is right to have slaves. Nor does this story raise the question of whether the master was kind to his servant. Jesus is simply taking an ordinary situation that would be familiar to all of His hearers and appealing to something that everyone would agree with. The slave is not doing the master a favor by serving him. It was part of his regular work to prepare the meal, or in any case it was part of his regular duty to do what the master commanded.

This story does not have to do with the question of whether a master should appreciate the earnest efforts of his slaves to please him. It simply emphasizes the fact that slaves are not thanked for doing what the master asks them to do in the way that a friend is thanked for a service rendered or for a favor bestowed. He has done his work and is still a humble slave, owned by the master and receiving all he has from the master.

The Spiritual Message (Luke 17:10)

What is the great central spiritual message of the parable? In what sense are we to be like this bondslave? For it is clear that we are to be as he is in *some* respect. A Christian may object that he does not want to consider himself either as a slave or as being unworthy. Did not our Lord say, "I no longer call you servants, because a servant does not know his master's business. Instead, I have called you friends, for everything that I learned from my Father I have made known to you" (John 15:15).

We must remember that in one sense we may be servants, or bondslaves, and in another sense we are not. Paul called himself the bondslave of Christ. Jesus told His disciples in what sense they were friends and not slaves; He had revealed the intimate secrets of the Father as He would do only to friends. So we are not to be bondslaves in the sense of being all that a slave is in relation to his master, but in some particular characteristic that may illustrate our relation to the Lord.

In the same way, Christians are called soldiers, or sheep, or children. In each case we need to study in what way we are to be like this or that; for we are to be children and are also exhorted to "no longer be infants" (Eph. 4:14), a different characteristic of children being in mind in each case.

In what sense are we to reckon ourselves unworthy slaves in the matter of Christian service? First of all, we have been bought with a price, the precious blood of Christ. Before we do one thing for God, He has done everything for us. He has emptied heaven, so to speak, in sending His beloved Son. The Father so loved the Son that He gave all things into His hand (John 3:35), and then He so loved us that He gave Christ to us. In giving Christ, He freely gave us all things.

It is quite evident, then, that whatever service we do for Christ we shall still be unworthy. We cannot earn anything from one who has first given us everything (Rom. 11:35-36). We begin our service for Christ having received salvation and all spiritual blessing as His free gift (Eph. 1:3). All service for such a Master will be done in grateful love; though we should do a thousand times more than we have done, we should still count ourselves unworthy servants and not suppose that we have given favors to God for which we deserve thanks.

Joined with this truth, there is a parallel truth: We cannot be better than good. We cannot do more than our duty. It is true that no Christian does perfectly all the things that are commanded him. But, our Lord says, if anyone should do all the things that are commanded him, he would still have done only that which is his duty to do.

The central message is that a Christian should serve in humble gratitude as a love-slave of a Master who first gave all for us and to us. We can render Him no "extra" service, for all we can possibly do is too little to show our love for such a Lord.

The Personal Application

If we have learned the truth of this parable, we shall approach our Christian ministry with a heart ready to be poured out in unstinted service. We belong wholly to the One who gave Himself for us. Men may be unreasonable and expect too much service from us. Men may be ungrateful and not recompense us properly in money or in other ways. But our service is done primarily for the Lord, and we never get weary in serving

Him, nor do we ever have the attitude that we have been unreasonably treated by Him or that extra service has been demanded of us.

Many a faithful pastor or missionary has been in the place where those to whom he ministered required much extra service and did not give him the material returns he should have had. He may recognize this and pray for the enlightenment of those who have mistreated him. But he will not weaken himself by self-pity. He will still know that he is an unworthy servant. He has done the things that were his duty to do, and he has done them for One who has paid so much for him that no service would ever recompense it.

In the same way, when a Christian worker has been wearied with a long day's work, or with repeated days' work, he will be happily ready for any call that may interrupt his rest, or his meals, or some cherished plan of his own. He will still know that he is not doing a favor to his Lord but will rejoice that he can serve in any way the One who has purchased him.

Again, this attitude in service will prevent our thinking of ourselves more highly than we ought to think. A Christian servant will never compare himself with others and judge that he has done extra service. This parable wholly eliminates the thought of works of supererogation, that is, works that give a position of special sainthood because there has been goodness beyond the requirement. There is no goodness of man's that even equals the requirements of God. We are not to compare ourselves with one another and congratulate ourselves because our record seems so much better than the record of certain others.

The teaching of this parable does not mean that the Lord does not reward us for our service. It does not mean that we work without any returns, or even without expecting returns. There are other glorious teachings concerning Christian service that are brought out in other parables. But this foundation truth should carry through all our service. We are serving Him who gave all for us, and we need the humble, grateful attitude of those who are redeemed by the priceless blood of Christ and upon whom has been showered the utmost love of God. We can never do enough for Him.

REVIEW OF LESSON 7

1. In what sense can Christians consider themselves "unworthy servants"?

2. What other verses in Scripture tell us that we are worthy?

3. What has Christ done for us as Christians that goes before any service we do for him?

4. Does this parable teach that we should work without expecting any reward?

5. Does this parable have anything to say to Christians who are serving in spite of inadequate pay? To Christians who are serving people who are ungrateful? To Christians who are doing more than should be expected of them?

PREPARATION FOR LESSON 8

Reading Lesson: Matthew 19:23–20:16

1. What is the setting of this story?

2. How many different classes of workers are mentioned in this parable, and what made the difference between them?

3. In your opinion, which parts of the story have spiritual significance?

4. Did the first group of workers have good reason for complaining?

5. Do you think this parable has any application to salvation?

Lesson 8

The Workers in the Vineyard

Matthew 20:1-16

The parable of the workers who labored but one hour and received the same wages as those who worked twelve hours has aroused special interest. Our natural sympathies go out to these men who worked hard all day, and we can understand their feeling that they should receive more. Many conflicting interpretations have been given to this parable.

We have included it as one of the four parables of service, judging that the primary message of the parable does not concern salvation but the matter of the right attitude in serving our Lord. It is true that salvation and Christian service are intimately related, and this parable grows out of a discussion concerning who will be saved and enter into the kingdom of heaven.

The Setting (Matt. 19:23-30)

On our Lord's last journey to Jerusalem, as recorded in Matthew 19 and 20, He dealt with three burning questions: divorce, the right attitude toward little children, and the Christian view of riches. In all three of these matters our Lord's teachings completely upset the standards of His day.

The standards of our own day on these matters are also in large measure utterly contrary to Christ's teachings.

The discussion concerning riches arose over the rich young man who eagerly ran to Christ desiring to know how he might inherit eternal life. The command to go and sell all that he had was a test to determine whether he was really keeping the commandment, "Love your neighbor as yourself," as he said he was.

When he went away sorrowful, our Lord stated: "It is hard for a rich man to enter the kingdom of heaven. Again I tell you, it is easier for a camel to go through the eye of a needle than for a rich man to enter the kingdom of God" (19:23-24). We read that the disciples "were greatly astonished and asked, 'Who then can be saved?'" (v. 25).

It is evident that people in those days had about the same view of riches that we have, namely, that rich people should receive special favor from man and God. Our Lord's answer went deeper than the import of their question: "With man this is impossible, but with God all things are possible" (v. 26). The salvation of anyone, poor or rich, is impossible apart from the miraculous power of God. His grace is able to save even a rich man.

Then Peter asked a very direct and personal question. The rich young man had refused to accept Christ's invitation, "Come, follow me" (v. 21). But Peter and the other apostles had left their worldly occupations and possessions at the call of Christ to follow Him (Matt. 4:19-22). It was natural that Peter should think of this contrast and ask his question. "We have left everything to follow you! What then will there be for us?" (19:27).

Our Lord gives two answers to this question. The parable we are studying is the second answer. Peter's question, therefore, is the setting of the parable and gives a key to understanding its central message.

First, our Lord answers Peter's question directly. "I tell you the truth, at the renewal of all things, when the Son of Man sits on his glorious throne, you who have followed me will also sit on twelve thrones, judging the twelve tribes of Israel" (v. 28). This surely is a reward exceeding all they had thought or imagined. These humble men of the people are to become the rulers of all Israel. How their hearts must have dwelt with keen anticipation on this promise.

As Christ drew near to the Cross, the disciples thought they were drawing near to these crowns. And they were not satisfied to sit on the throne but were discussing the degree of greatness each would have. Our Lord taught them that He was in the midst as one who serves. They were to be great in humility and self-sacrificial in service.

Then He added, "You are those who have stood by me in my trials. And I confer on you a kingdom, just as my Father conferred one on me, so that you may eat and drink at my table in my kingdom and sit on thrones, judging the twelve tribes of Israel" (Luke 22:28-30). As the four hundred who went without the camp to serve David in his exile became rulers with him when he came into the kingdom, so those who suffer with Christ will reign with Him.

Our Lord adds a further word in this first answer to Peter's question. Evidently there is a special sense in which the twelve apostles are to occupy twelve thrones. This is a peculiar honor not open to all Christians. But Christ adds: "And everyone who has left houses or brothers or sisters or father or mother or children or fields for my sake will receive a hundred times as much and will inherit eternal life" (Matt. 19:29).

That is a large increase on the investment. In this present life they will receive a hundredfold, which is ten thousand percent, in addition to becoming the heirs of eternal life. God will never be debtor to any man, and He will not deal with us as we deserve, but infinitely beyond that.

But it was necessary that a second answer be given to Peter's question. Their minds would naturally turn to those thrones and not to the service and suffering that lay before them, as is evidenced by their disputes as to who should be greatest (Mark 10:37; Luke 9:46; 22:24). So our Lord added the statement, "But many who are first will be last, and many who are last will be first" (Matt. 19:30), thereby illustrating what He meant by the parable of the workers in the vineyard. The parable is intended as a gentle rebuke to Peter for the spirit of his question, and it gives instruction on the right attitude in service.

The Story (Matt. 20:1-15)

A landowner goes out to the marketplace early in the morning, that is, about six o'clock, to hire workers. He makes a bargain as to wages and agrees to pay each of these workers one denarius for their day's work. This was the wage often paid for a day's work in that time. At the third, sixth, and ninth hour, that is, at nine, twelve, and three o'clock, he goes out and hires others, telling them, "I will pay you whatever is right." These groups went to work in the vineyard not trusting to an agreement but trusting to the promise of their employer to deal with them fairly.

About the eleventh hour, an hour before sundown, he went out and found others standing and asked them, "Why have you been standing here all day long doing nothing?" They replied, "Because no one has hired us." Notice that no blame is attached to the men for standing all the day idle. They were in the marketplace, and as the various landowners came they were passed by and not hired. Or perhaps they had not been in that particular place all the day.

The story does not go into these details, but no point should be made of the fact that they stood idle all day, as though they were not willing to work. The landowner told them to go into the vineyard. He made no agreement and gave them no promise. These last went to work trusting to the fairness of the man who hired them.

Then comes the unusual part of the story. We have said that parable stories are true to life. This does not mean that they may not tell unusual things. They are true to life in the sense that what happens in the parable could happen in real life though it might be an unusual thing.

Those hired last were paid first. How surprised they must have been, and overjoyed, when every man received a full day's wages! They had no complaint against this generous master. All the others who worked part of a day received a full day's pay, and they likewise made no complaint. The lord had told them that whatever was right he would give them, and he gave them more than their just due.

Those who came first and worked for the twelve hours took eager notice of what all the others received, doubtless listening to the delighted exclamations of surprise. They waited to know how much more they should receive. In their disappointment at receiving the same amount, the day's wages they had bargained for, they protested to the landowner. "These men who were hired last worked only one hour, and you have made them equal to us who have borne the burden of the work and the heat of the day."

Not only had these others worked but one-twelfth of the time, but they had also worked during the pleasantest hour of the day, while the first group worked long hours right through the scorching heat. The master gives them a conclusive answer that closes their lips to any further complaint.

Addressing one of them, perhaps the leader of the group, he answered: "Friend, I am not being unfair to you. Didn't you agree to work for a denarius? Take your pay and go. I want to give the man who was hired last the same as I gave you. Don't I have a right to do what I want with my own money?"

He reminds them of the bargain they had made. They were working under an agreement, and they received absolute justice. No wrong had been done them, and they surely would have to agree that the lord had a right to use his money as he pleased since he had been entirely fair to them.

The landowner adds a question that goes to the heart of what was wrong with these workers: "Or are you envious because I am generous?" This landowner was just to those who had worked twelve hours and was more than just, indeed very generous, to those who had worked but one hour.

When we read that God is good, it does not ordinarily refer to God's holiness and perfection but to the fact that He is full of mercy and loving-kindness. God is good to Israel, and God is good to all. So when we read that Barnabas was a good man (Acts 11:24), it does not refer to his excellent Christian character, though he had that, but to the fact that he was a large-hearted and generous Christian. The fruit of the Spirit is "goodness," which does not mean uprightness in general but this quality of generosity, showing mercy and loving-kindness to others, giving even as God gives.

The Spiritual Message (Matt. 20:16)

Noted Bible scholars and Bible teachers have given varying interpretations to this parable, including the following:

- The various bands of workers are the Old Testament saints; those called at the eleventh hour are the apostles.
- The workers first called are the Jews; those called last are the Gentiles.
- It is a warning not to be overconfident even though we have begun our Christian course well.
- In the matter of salvation all are equal, since all are saved by grace through faith.

- The parable represents the whole gospel age up to Christ's return, and the workers are the groups saved at various periods.
- It refers to the period in a man's life in which he begins to serve the Lord, some in infancy, others in youth, others in manhood, others in old age; and the parable encourages those who enter late on God's field of service to labor heartily.

The only explanation of the meaning of the parable recorded in the Gospel is in the words of our Lord: "So the last will be first, and the first will be last" (Matt. 20:16). He is here repeating the words that introduce the parable but giving them in a condensed form. He does not mean that *all* the last will be first, nor all the first last, but (as in 19:30) *many* will be last that are first. That is, there will be a reason why the first are last and the last first.

There is a direct application of this statement to the apostles, who were first called into fellowship with the Lord. There would be the natural danger not only that they should be puffed up by this distinction but also that they should fail to see the need of personal responsibility in making their service what it ought to be. But while the first application is to them, the principle of the right Christian attitude in life and service applies to all believers.

It is clear that one purpose of this parable is to rebuke whatever of a wrong attitude was evidenced by Peter's question, "What are we going to get?" This is a natural question when men are sacrificing some present good or doing some service. It is perfectly right when men are being employed that they should have an agreement as to what wages are to be paid.

In the parable story the workers made a contract, or agreement, to work for a certain amount. These first workers, who spent the whole day in the service, were working under a legal agreement, and they were working for wages rather than for the joy of the work, or for delight in what they accomplished, or for the love of their employer.

In the story there is no blame attached to these men for making an agreement. It was the natural thing to do. Later they did display a wrong spirit in murmuring against the man who employed them. They represent the servants of God who have their eye on the wages or the reward. They ask, "What are we going to get?"

Many have drawn the conclusion that Christians should serve without any thought of wages or reward. They teach, for example, that it is a wrong principle to offer rewards to children in Sunday school. But the fact is that this parable and other parables, as well as other teachings in the Word, tell us plainly that Christians are to look toward great future reward as an encouragement to present zeal and steadfastness.

The men who were hired at the third, sixth, and ninth hours went into the vineyard to work trusting to the promise of the employer that he would give them what was right. They also were expecting a return for their labor, but they had made no specific agreement. Had the landowner paid them only half of what was rightfully theirs, they would have had no legal redress. He might have said that was his view of what was just.

Those who were hired at the eleventh hour went into the field with no promise from the lord. This does not mean that they expected no remuneration for their service. It means they trusted that matter entirely to the master who was employing them. They were surprised to receive twelve times as much as was their due.

The central truth, therefore, is that we should serve our Lord without being concerned about what we will get in return, knowing that He who first of all gave Himself before we had done any service will reward us abundantly above all that we think. Our Lord delights to give overflowingly and abundantly. When He gives life, He gives abundant, overflowing life. When He rewards for service, He gives ten thousand percent now in this life and in the age to come such wonders of eternal life as cannot even be imagined.

But He can deal in this way only with those who trust Him. If men insist upon justice, then He must give them justice. If men serve with a mercenary spirit, then He cannot pour out generous gifts upon them.

The parable story is not teaching that all who are saved, are saved by grace with no distinction. If this were the teaching, there would be no distinction between those who worked twelve hours and the others; but it is clear that those men who worked twelve hours showed a covetous and complaining spirit and a jealousy against those whom the master favored. Their feelings were entirely natural from the human standpoint. But our Lord is seeking to unfold a new world of relationship to a new Master that will be utterly different from all the standards of the world.

All believers will be equal in that their sins are forgiven and that they are made holy in Christ. But as one star differs from another in glory, so it will be in the resurrection (1 Cor. 15:41-42); and this seems to indicate that there will be differences among those who are saved. Some who are first, that is, those who, like the apostles, appear to have great advantage over others, may by their failure to enter into Christ's secret of service, lose that first place. Others who for whatever reason seem to have a place of obscurity in the kingdom of God may by their zeal attain a high place.

The parable is continuing the instruction concerning the contrast between serving earthly masters and serving the Lord. The great ones among the Gentiles exercise authority over them and each seeks to be the greatest. But in the kingdom of God the greatest is the one who is the greatest servant; the one who has the first place is the one who takes the lowest place.

This is what our Lord did. He went to the lowest depths of shame and is now exalted to the highest heights of glory. As the Master, so is the servant to be. Christ never served in the spirit of "What can I get out of it?" He committed Himself to the Father who gave Him the highest place.

This is what our Lord, speaking now of Him as the Son of Man, obtained from the Father. He did not serve under any agreement to obtain this. So it should be our desire to be chief among the servants. We should be afraid of the temptations to seek great things for ourselves and to inquire about how much we are to get out of all our sacrifice and self-denial.

The Personal Application

It is well to distinguish between the central truth of the parable and the various applications that may be made. Some have said that the workers who labored twelve hours represent the Jews. It is quite true that the Jews as a whole did serve in a legal spirit. A remnant from the Jews understood the new order of the kingdom of God. Those who came in the eleventh hour are spoken of as the Gentiles.

It would seem quite reasonable to regard this as one application of the truth but not to suppose that the parable was primarily given to teach this. Not only the Jews, but any who work under a legal agreement, will receive all that is due them, whether it be in the matter of a lost man who is seeking to win salvation by his works or a Christian who is losing the fruit of his service because of a wrong attitude.

Another application has suggested Paul as one who came in at the eleventh hour. He labored more than all the apostles. He took a place higher than those who originally were called. This also is an application of the truth of the parable. Every one of the apostles had the opportunity to work with as great zeal as Paul showed.

But the application of the truth of the parable is to every

Christian in every age. One may be called to a service of sowing, another to the glad labor of reaping. One may spend a lifetime in a foreign field with little fruit, another may reap the Lord's harvest in evangelistic work and in sweeping revivals. One may have a long lifetime of sowing and reaping for Christ's glory, another may be cut off in the midst of glorious service.

One may serve in a time of spiritual quickening, another at a time when men are turning from God. One in an age of tolerance, another in the midst of terrible persecution. One in the darkness of the Middle Ages, another in the light of the Reformation. One in a period of reverence for God and His Word, another in the great apostasy when men turn from faith in God.

The parable is not intended to specify various differences of this sort. Whoever the servant, and whatever the time or conditions of his service, he is to labor in the joy of his Lord, committing entirely to Him the question of what he shall have for his labor and zeal.

Paul was pressing home this same glorious truth when he wrote to the Ephesians and the Colossians. He told the household slaves of that time to serve their masters in singleness of heart just as if they were serving Christ.

> Obey them not only to win their favor when their eye is on you, but like slaves of Christ, doing the will of God from your heart. Serve wholeheartedly, as if you were serving the Lord, not men, because you know that the Lord will reward everyone for whatever good he does, whether he is slave or free. (Eph. 6:6-8)

How truly marvelous this is, that whatever work those Christian slaves were doing was service to the Lord. Not merely when they were testifying to their heathen neighbors concerning Christ, but also when they were carrying out the commands of heathen masters, perhaps ungrateful or hard masters, they were serving Christ. They were looking to Him for their real wages. Knowing what kind of a paymaster the Lord is, they need not be troubled about the earthly recompense or the lack of appreciation on the part of earthly masters. How such a spirit would transform life and service!

REVIEW OF LESSON 8

1. What is the spiritual significance of the fact that the employer had a different agreement with each of the three groups of workers?

2. How might this parable apply to the twelve apostles? To the Jews? To Paul?

3. What is the central message of this parable?

4. How is this central message related to the first being last and the last first?

5. How might this parable inspire us to greater Christian service?

PREPARATION FOR LESSON 9

Reading Lesson: Matthew 25:14-30. Read also Matthew 24:1–25:13.

1. What reward did the first two servants receive?
2. What is the spiritual truth of this?
3. What, do you think, is the central message of this parable?
4. What is taught here concerning the second coming of Christ?
5. What is the relationship between Christ's second coming and Christian service?

The Talents

Matthew 25:14-30

An additional and distinctly new teaching concerning the secret of effective service is given in the parable of the talents. This is one of the most familiar of our Lord's parables, and it has given a new word to the English language, or rather a new meaning to the word *talent.*

The parable of the unworthy servant teaches us to begin all our Christian service with the knowledge that we are serving Him who has given all for us and that we can never repay Him or do enough to show our gratitude. Yet the Lord does give us a return for our service, and the second parable of service studied, that of the workers in the vineyard, teaches us that since we are serving such a Lord we commit entirely to Him the question of what returns will come, knowing that He will give us abundantly more than we deserve. The parable of the talents gives a teaching concerning the basis on which our Lord will reward us for faithful service.

The Setting (Matt. 24:1–25:13)

It is significant that this parable of the talents, a parable on Christian service, is in the midst of teaching concerning the personal return of our Lord. This is Christ's famous farewell discourse on the Mount of Olives in which He predicts the destruction of Jerusalem and the signs that will precede His personal return. He concludes this part of the message with the command: "Therefore keep watch, because you do not know on what day your Lord will come" (Matt. 24:42). In the midst of the address, He gives them the parable-simile of the fig tree putting forth its leaves. Following the discourse He gives them four parables or parable-similes: watching against the thief; the faithful and wicked servants waiting for their lord; the ten virgins; and the talents.

His address concludes with a picture of the judgment and the separation of the sheep from the goats. The parable of the ten virgins concludes with the application: "Therefore keep watch, because you do not know the day or the hour" (25:13). Then the parable of the talents begins. So this parable is closely linked with the teaching to watch for the return of the Lord. In the story of the virgins, they were waiting for the bridegroom; in the story of the talents, the servants were working for their lord during his absence. The message, therefore, must concern the service of Christians from the time our Lord left the earth until He personally returns and calls His servants to an accounting.

The Story (Matt. 25:14-30)

We have said that parable stories are true to life. This means that they are true to the life of that time, and it is necessary to study the historical background to understand this story. The slaves of that day not only did ordinary work for their masters, they would also engage in business for him, perhaps sharing in the profit. This story is perhaps an unusual illustration of that practice.

The master goes into another country and evidently leaves all of his goods, or his entire capital, to his bondslaves for them to carry on in his absence. Three servants are taken as representing all. To one of these he gives five talents. The word "talent" has the sense of "weight," and the talent referred to here is thought to be equivalent to about thirty-three hundred day's wages. In modern times, using twenty-five dollars as a daily wage, these five talents would be worth more than four hundred thousand dollars. This servant therefore had considerable capital to work with.

We use the word *talent* today to refer to the special ability or aptitude one may have, as, for example, a talent for music or art. And this meaning of the word comes from this parable. But in Jesus' time, "talent" meant money—the capital the servants were using. These servants received differing amounts according to their ability. Today, too, we observe that one person can be productive with a large sum of money, whereas another struggles to put a much smaller amount to good use.

The servant who received five talents and the servant who received two went *at once* and traded with them, and each doubled his original capital. The servant who received one talent did not attempt to trade with it but dug a hole in the earth and hid his master's money. It was the custom in those days to bury treasure, as in the parable of the man who found treasure hid in a field (Matt. 13:44).

The master stayed away a long time. Perhaps some of the servants wondered if he would ever come back. But he did return, and then came the time of reckoning. With joy the servants who had gained talents made their reports. To each the master said exactly the same words: "Well done, good and faithful servant! You have been faithful with a few things; I will put you in charge of many things. Come and share your master's happiness!"

There is first personal commendation from the master; then the reward of added responsibility, lordship over many things, whereas the thousands of dollars they had been handling were considered "few things"; and third, as a climax of the reward, this new responsibility was to be in the joy of their master, who now was not to go away again into another country but to stay with them.

The man who received the single talent also came to report. He was not dishonest; he wanted to return his master's money. He also wanted to justify himself for hiding the money and not attempting to trade with it. His justification is in effect a condemnation of his master.

Knowing that the master was a "hard man," reaping the fruit of others' labors when he himself was not laboring, gathering what others had earned for him, the servant said he was afraid. He was probably afraid that he might lose the money and be reprimanded by his master. He told of having hid the talent in the earth and then concluded, explaining, "See, here is what belongs to you." He thought this finished the matter because he had stolen nothing from his master and had returned what had been given to him.

The reprimand for this servant was as severe as the master's commendation of the others was glorious. He called the others "good and faithful" servants. This one is "a wicked and lazy servant," the opposite of good and faithful. The reasons the servant gave for his failure were false. The real reasons were his selfishness and laziness. He was wicked in the sense of being false-hearted toward his master, and this was expressed in his laziness.

If it were really true that he thought his master was a hard man, reaping where he did not sow, then he would have known that he would require his money with interest. The servant really did not return what his master had entrusted to him. Money buried in the earth is making its owner poorer by the day.

But as a matter of fact, the master was not that kind of

overseer. He did not want the talent. He wanted his servant to be faithful. He does not honor the attempt to return the talent. He takes it away from the wicked servant and gives to the one who had the ten talents. The master then quotes the proverb, "For everyone who has will be given more, and he will have an abundance. Whoever does not have, even what he has will be taken from him."

The loss of the talent is not the only loss sustained by the lazy servant. His master adds, "And throw that worthless servant outside, into the darkness, where there will be weeping and gnashing of teeth."

Note that we are still studying the parable story. The faithful servants were first of all commended by their master; they were called "good and faithful" servants. The other servant was condemned; he was called "a wicked and lazy servant." The faithful servants had the reward of being set over many things. The unfaithful servant had even his original capital taken from him. The climax of the blessedness of the other servants was that they should enter into their master's joy. The climax of the loss of the unprofitable servant was that he lost the joy of his master. This is figuratively expressed as being thrown into darkness, where there is the weeping and gnashing of teeth.

The Spiritual Message

No explanation of the parable is added by our Lord. We are to find the meaning in the story itself. The man going into another country represents our Lord leaving this earth and going to the right hand of the Father.

The words "after a long time the master of those servants returned" clearly indicate that a long time would elapse before the return of the Lord. Unbelieving critics have frequently asserted that the apostles expected Christ to return in their generation and that the apostles, therefore, were mistaken.

The apostles did teach that Christians were to be ever ready for the Lord's return and were to be in an expectant attitude. But far from teaching that He would return in their lifetime, there are strong indications that the whole program of the gospel message pointed to a long period.

It is true that a generation might appear a long period to a suffering servant; and it is not the intention of our Lord, or of the Holy Spirit through the apostles, to indicate what the length of time will be. Already it has been many centuries, and we can see that this was suggested in the expression "after a long time."

The servants represent those who call Jesus "Lord," that is, the professing Christians. All such are called to be servants of Christ.

The talents represent not the special abilities of the servants of Christ but the capital He gives them to work with, that is, the opportunities for service, together with all their material, personal, and spiritual gifts. With Christ, God has freely given us all things, and He has given us the Holy Spirit that He might take of these things of Christ and reveal them to us. Thus, in giving us the Holy Spirit, He gives us all things necessary for our life and service.

We should take special note of the blessed truth that God gives opportunities and equipment in accordance with our ability. The talents represent not only opportunities but responsibilities. But He does not make any Christian responsible for service that he cannot, by God's grace, perform.

Christians differ in their gifts and abilities. God does not call a man who cannot carry a tune to be a singing evangelist. Nor does He call a talented musician who is slow of speech to be a preacher. Ordinarily a great executive is not at the same time a great philosopher. A poet is not usually a good theologian. Some with the gift for being a poet or a teacher or an executive have entered the theological field and made shipwreck of their own service and of the faith of many others. How good of our Lord that He gives us capital exactly adapted to what we are enabled by His grace to do.

We need to remember that it is the Lord Himself who knows just what abilities we have. When William Carey gave himself for missionary service, he expected to go to the South Sea Islands. But the Lord called him to India, where he became one of the greatest linguists of his day, mastering the many languages of highly cultured India for the kingdom of God's sake. The cobbler did not know he had these gifts. The Lord put him into the greatest field in the world for the exercise of those gifts.

Livingstone thought of China as the mission field where he should serve, but God saw in Livingstone the gifts that made him a great pioneer and explorer. There was one great field for such gifts—the dark, unexplored continent of Africa. God placed him there. What a glory to yield our lives to One who knows us altogether and knows the world and knows the very place where we belong, whether for obscure or prominent service.

The return of the master and his reckoning with his servants clearly points to the personal return of Christ, when all Christians will appear before Him. This is the time, we are distinctly told, "for rewarding your servants the prophets and your saints and those who reverence your name, both small and great—and for destroying those who destroy the earth" (Rev. 11:18).

We often speak of Christians going to their reward at death. It is true that Christians then go into the presence of the Lord and that is joy unspeakable. But this is not the time when Christ reckons with them as to the faithfulness of their service. Paul said, "For what is our hope, our joy, or the crown in which we will glory in the presence of our Lord Jesus when he comes? Is it not you?" (1 Thess. 2:19). Death is never portrayed as the goal or climax of the Christian's life. Rather, our Lord looks at Christian service as continuing from the time of His ascension until His return, just as though the same group of servants were working.

This parable, like a number of other portions of Scripture, does not have to do with the time of this judgment nor does it distinguish between the first resurrection and the resurrection that will follow a thousand years later (Rev. 20:5-6). Frequently in Scripture that whole thousand-year period is reckoned as the day of the Lord or the day of judgment, with certain great events taking place at the beginning and at the end. But these questions do not affect the spiritual message of this parable: Every professing Christian will appear before the judgment seat of Christ, and the faithfulness or unfaithfulness of our service will be judged. It is evident that this parable does not concern salvation, except as faithful service may be an indication of real discipleship.

The central truth of the parable, so far as the faithful servants are concerned, is this: Equal rewards for equal faithfulness in service. A steward must be faithful. The man receiving the two talents was not responsible for making five talents or for attempting things that could only be done by a man having five talents. He was as faithful in his use of two talents as was the more gifted servant in his use of five. To both of them our Lord will say, "Well done, good and faithful servant." Both of them will be set over many things. That is, part of the reward is increased activity and responsibility in serving our wonderful Savior.

But what of the man who buried his talent? He represents an unfaithful servant. He is a professing Christian who has called Christ Lord. He has not been wicked in the sense of doing things against his Lord. He has been false and lazy in what he has failed to do. This is a man who takes the name of Christ but does nothing in the way of bearing fruit for the

Lord. It has been suggested that the fact that he has but one talent is a temptation to him to suppose that it matters little whether he makes use of his small capital. But our Lord is not treating him unfairly. The man with the greater gifts has proportionately greater responsibilities.

Does this unprofitable servant represent a professing Christian who is not saved? His being cast into the outer darkness where there is weeping and gnashing of teeth would seem to indicate that he is. But in that case the parable would suggest that every saved person is a faithful servant, that only those will be saved to whom our Lord can say, "Well done, good and faithful servant." (This would not mean that their good and faithful service would save them but rather that those who are saved by grace through faith in Christ would indicate it by fruit in their lives.) If this interpretation is held to strictly, it would mean that no unfaithful Christian will be saved.

But other Scriptures indicate that there are Christians who are born again and yet are unfaithful in their ministry— Christians who will be ashamed to stand before our Lord at His coming. So John urged, "And now, dear children, continue in Him, so that when he appears we may be confident and unashamed before him at his coming" (1 John 2:28). This warning is probably related to Paul's message to the Corinthians concerning building on the one foundation that is laid—namely, Jesus Christ.

> If any man builds on this foundation using gold, silver, costly stones, wood, hay or straw, his work will be shown for what it is, because the Day will bring it to light. It will be revealed with fire, and the fire will test the quality of each man's work. If what he has built survives, he will receive his reward. If it is burned up, he will suffer loss; he himself will be saved, but only as one escaping through the flames. (1 Cor. 3:12-15)

This passage, it is true, primarily applies to Christian ministers, but its principle applies to all servants of Christ who are building on the one foundation of Christ. The teaching is that all service of a believer that is not done in the Spirit of God will be burned away, and that a Christian may have all his work burned up while he himself is saved.

To the same intent is Paul's testimony concerning his own eagerness for faithful service:

> So we make it our goal to please him, whether we are at home in the body or away from it. For we must all appear before the judgment seat of Christ, that each one may receive what is due him for the things done while in the body, whether good or bad. (2 Cor. 5:9–10)

It is doubtless significant that "judgment seat" here is *bema*, the name of the place for the judges at the Greek games. These judges rated the athletes and gave them their rewards. This is not referring to the judgment for sin. It is true that the good things Christians do indicate that they have been born again, and the bad lives that others live indicate that they have not taken Christ as their Savior; but there is also the judgment concerning the way we have behaved as Christians and the measure of our faithfulness in service.

Paul also wrote:

> Do you not know that in a race all the runners run, but only one gets the prize? Run in such a way as to get the prize. Everyone who competes in the games goes into strict training. They do it to get a crown that will not last; but we do it to get a crown that will last forever. Therefore I do not run like a man running aimlessly; I do not fight like a man beating the air. No, I beat my body and make it my slave so that after I have preached to others, I myself will not be disqualified for the prize. (1 Cor. 9:24-27)

Paul is not speaking of salvation, although it is evidence of his salvation that he is striving for the incorruptible crown. He does not want to be "disqualified," as the runners might be in the Greek games, and thereby lose the prize.

To come back to the message of the parable, it is clear that these unfaithful servants represent professing Christians. It is also clear that there are professing Christians unfaithful in service who have never been born again. But there are also Christians who are on the foundation of Christ Jesus and yet are building wood, hay, and stubble on that foundation. They are unfaithful servants. They will suffer loss, or damage. We judge, then, that the servant in the parable may be either lost or saved.

In any case, the warning of the parable is against unfaithfulness in service. If one is an unprofitable servant, there is no evidence to others or to himself that he is really saved. It is characteristic of these warnings of our Lord that He does not seek to distinguish between the unfaithful ones who may be saved and those who may be mere professors. The warning is given that the truly saved ones may turn from their unfaithfulness and that those who are not saved may be constrained to find Christ.

But what would casting into outer darkness mean for a saved person who has been an unfaithful servant? This figure is part of the story only. It is a vivid warning against the terrible loss resulting from unfaithfulness but not necessarily a picture of eternal hell. There will be distinctions in heaven, though all Christians will be equally cleansed and will have the joy of salvation. There will be no weeping and gnashing of teeth there. This, however, applies to the eternal state, about which the Scriptures tell us little, except to indicate something of its exceeding glory.

The Scriptures do say that the saints are to reign with Christ for a thousand years of the kingdom age (Rev. 20:4). We may judge that, somewhat as the invisible host of angels serve the Lord today, ministering to the heirs of salvation, the saints will share with Christ in His judging and ruling of the earth, doing services such as angels are doing now.

That is, the resurrected saints will not be living on earth as they once did but will be reigning with Christ. The service in that period will depend on their faithfulness now, and it is quite possible that the unfaithful servants, while they rejoice in their salvation, will also have the reward of their unfaithfulness in not sharing in those services that might have been theirs in this kingdom age. Instead there will be tears of regret, which will be wiped away in the new heaven and new earth (Rev. 21:4).

The Personal Application

But since the Scriptures tell us little as to life and service during the millennial period or kingdom age, we need not speculate. The practical appeal of the parable is clear. It is a great stimulus to faithfulness in service, knowing of the sure and glorious reward, and a warning against laziness, knowing of the sure and unspeakable loss.

REVIEW OF LESSON 9

1. What does the fact that different amounts were given to each of the servants teach concerning Christian service?

2. In what way may the sin of the man with one talent represent a professing Christian who is not saved?

3. In what way may he represent an unfaithful Christian?

4. Does this parable suggest anything with regard to the time of Christ's second coming? What bearing does this have on Christian service?

5. Should Christians work for rewards?

PREPARATION FOR LESSON 10

Reading Lesson: Luke 19:11-27

1. In what way does this parable differ from the parable of the talents?

2. In what way is it similar?

3. In what part of His ministry did Christ speak this parable?

4. Why did He speak this parable?

5. What does the master going into a far country to receive a kingdom represent? Whom do the citizens represent?

Lesson 10

The Ten Minas

Luke 19:12-27

The parable of the minas is quite distinct from the parable of the talents, and it also has an added message concerning Christian service. The similarities in the two parables have led some Bible scholars to consider them different reports of the same parable, but we can establish that each of them is distinct.

First, the parable of the minas was spoken to the multitudes, before Christ entered Jerusalem. The parable of the talents was spoken to the apostles only, and this took place several days after Christ had entered Jerusalem. Second, in the parable of the minas there were ten servants, and each received one mina. In the parable of the talents there were three servants, and they received a different number of talents. Third, in the parable of the minas there are the additional factors of citizens who do not want their master to reign over them and a nobleman who goes into a far country and comes back a king. And fourth, the currency is a distinguishing feature—one talent was sixty times more valuable than one mina.

These and other details indicate that these two parables are distinct, and therefore we can conclude that each teaches a distinct spiritual truth. The similarities in the two parables indicate that both teach great principles of Christian service.

The Setting (Luke 19:11)

A notable feature of the Gospel of Luke is the great passage from 9:51 to 19:28, usually called the Perean section. Many of the events and teachings recorded here—including fifteen parables—are found only in this Gospel. It covers the period of our Lord's ministry between the close of His Galilean ministry—when He set His face to go to Jerusalem—and the beginning of His last week on earth. Chapters 19 and 20 in Matthew and chapter 10 in Mark are given to this period. In Luke this section closes with the parable of the minas. Each of the Synoptic Gospels next describes the triumphal entry into Jersusalem.

The setting of the parable is given in one verse, and it is striking. "While they were listening to this, he went on to tell them a parable, because he was near Jerusalem and the people thought that the kingdom of God was going to appear at once" (Luke 19:11).

We need to keep in mind that all Palestine had been aroused by the teaching that the kingdom of God was at hand. The message of John the Baptist, of Christ, and of the apostles dealt with this kingdom of God, or kingdom of heaven.

John sent his famous question as to whether Jesus was the One who was to come or whether they were to look for another because our Lord was fulfilling His gracious ministry of salvation but there seemed to be no signs of the fire of judgment. Perhaps in John's view the unfruitful trees were not being cut down and the chaff was not being burned up with unquenchable fire. The time of judgment, joined with the time of the glorious reign of Christ, was still future. John did not know this, nor did the disciples of Christ.

When our Lord entered Jerusalem, both the great multitude following Him and His apostles were expecting Him to be crowned king. In spite of His clear prediction that He would be put to death by the rulers, the disciples did not understand. They were looking forward to the setting up of an earthly kingdom at Jerusalem. This is why they were contending as to who should be greatest. This is why the mother of John and James came with her sons to ask that they might have the places of honor at the right and left hand of Christ when He came in His kingdom.

When it is said, therefore, that they thought the kingdom of God was to appear immediately, it means that they thought He would be accepted by the nation, crowned as king, and would set up the glorious theocratic kingdom prophesied in the Old Testament. The Lord gave the parable of the ten minas to correct this false impression.

He was to be crowned at Jerusalem, but with a crown of thorns. He was to be lifted up by the rulers of the people, but lifted up on a cross. He was to be crowned with glory and honor after this suffering of death. But we still do not see all things put under Him, and His coming into His kingdom is still a future matter (Heb. 2:7-10).

Nothing could be clearer than the fact that our Lord did not deny that the kingdom of God was to come on earth. He never hestitated to correct any false impressions of His followers. As He Himself said, "If it were not so, I would have told you" (John 14:2). If there was not to be an earthly kingdom, He would have told them plainly. Instead of telling them that, He gave them a parable to indicate that the earthly kingdom would be set up, but not immediately.

As the nobleman went into the distant country to receive a kingdom and to return, so our Lord was to go away from the earth but was to return again for the purpose of establishing the kingdom of God on earth. This multitude had many mistaken notions of what that kingdom would be, but their belief that the kingdom would be set up on earth with Jerusalem as the center was not of their own imagination but was what the Old Testament prophets predicted and what our Lord Jesus Christ plainly confirmed. The parable gives the message as to how Christians are to act in the period between the going away and the return of their King.

After the resurrection of our Lord, the disciples asked the question, "Are you at this time going to restore the kingdom to Israel?" (Acts 1:6). Our Lord did not tell them that they were mistaken about the kingdom being restored to Israel. As a matter of fact, He had been talking to them from time to time during the forty days after His resurrection concerning the kingdom of God (Acts 1:3).

It is unthinkable that He should not have corrected any false notions about an earthly kingdom. His answer plainly implied that the kingdom is to be restored to Israel but that the question of when it will happen is one that the disciples should not be concerned about. Their part was to go forth, after the Holy Spirit came upon them, to witness of their Savior to the ends of the earth.

The Story (Luke 19:12-27)

The story of a nobleman who went into a far country to receive a kingdom was strikingly illustrated in the case of Archelaus. There is little doubt that our Lord had this incident in mind. The parables, we have seen, are true to life and might even be based on actual events.

Herod the Great made his son Archelaus the ruler of Judea, with the title of king. Archelaus went to Rome to visit the emperor and to be confirmed as king. He was a tyrant and was unpopular in Judea. Some of his subjects sent a communication to the emperor requesting that he be removed from the kingdom and that Judea be placed under direct Roman government. Augustus assigned to him Judea, Samaria, and Idumea and gave him the title of ethnarch.

The nobleman in this story called ten of his bondservants and gave each one a mina, worth one hundred denarii; the mina would thus be worth perhaps twenty-five hundred dollars in modern times. Some suppose that this relatively small amount indicates the poverty of the nobleman; but evidently his purpose was to test the faithfulness and capacity of his servants rather than to have them earn money for him. The citizens are distinguished from the nobleman's own servants, and this feature does not appear in the parable of the talents.

Of the ten servants, three are used as illustrations. The one who gained ten minas from his one mina was given authority over ten cities in the new kingdom of the nobleman. The one who gained five minas was put over five cities. To the first the master said, "Well done, my good servant." These words are not repeated to the second servant, and this omission may have significance.

We read that the third servant kept the mina in a piece of cloth, like the servant in the parable of the talents who had buried his talent. And this servant gives a similar reason for not investing the mina—he was afraid that his master was an austere man.

The master, now a king, answers, "I will judge you by your own words, you wicked servant." That is, he would judge him according to his own statement, even though that statement was not true. If the servant had really respected his master's austerity, he would have invested the money, since the master would never have been satisfied with the mere return of the principal. The only punishment indicated for this unfaithful servant was that the mina was taken from him and given to the servant with ten minas.

Those nearby exclaimed, "Sir, . . . he already has ten!"

The master answers them with a proverb. "To everyone who has, more will be given, but as for the one who has nothing, even what he has will be taken away."

And the story then closes with the judgment on the citizens who did not want this man as their king.

The Spiritual Message

The central message of the parable of the talents is that there will be equal rewards for equal faithfulness in Christian service and terrible loss for unfaithfulness in service. The central message of the parable of the minas is that there will be different rewards for different degrees of diligence and zeal in service, with loss for unfaithfulness in service and destruction for those who renounce Christ as Lord and King.

Like the other parables, especially the longer ones, nearly all of the events of the story have a spiritual significance. Yet all of them center in the great truth concerning faithful service for the absent Lord.

The nobleman in the parable represents our Lord. It is not relevant here that Archelaus, or any other human ruler who went into a far country to receive a kingdom, was a wicked man and that his citizens might have reason to reject him. This detail about Archelaus has no bearing on the parable story.

In interpreting this parable we should picture Jesus at the right hand of the Father, waiting for the time of His return and the entering into His kingdom. This truth is taught by Peter in his sermon in Solomon's Colonnade, after healing the lame man at the gate of the temple (Acts 3:19-21). Heaven, the far country of the parable, has received the Lord Jesus until the time when the kingdom of God is to be set up on earth, that kingdom the disciples mistakenly thought would immediately appear when our Lord entered Jerusalem.

In each of the four parables of service we have studied we

see that our Lord is absent from us insofar as His bodily presence is concerned, and He has committed His work to us His servants, telling us to do this work until He comes. This does not contradict the glorious truth that the Lord Himself is with us until the consummation of the age (Matt. 28:19-20). Christ does not leave us the way in which the master in these parables left their servants. And without Him we can do nothing. It is His life working in and through us that bears fruit (John 15:1-8).

When our Lord does return, He will need servants to exercise authority in His kingdom, just as this nobleman needed faithful servants to set over the cities in his kingdom. Think of the difference between twenty-five hundred dollars—the approximate value of one mina in modern times—and ten cities in the kingdom.

Here is the principle of the vast difference between the "few things" for which we are responsible here and the many things in the kingdom of Christ that may become our responsibility. In earthly affairs, employers recognize that employees who are faithful in small matters will be faithful in much larger responsibilities. This same principle applies to all Christian service. However important our service here on earth may be, it is as nothing compared to our responsibilities in the future age. This applies to heaven and to all eternity, but there is evidently also a specific application to the kingdom age when our Lord will rule over the kingdoms of this earth during the millennium.

In the parable of the talents, a different amount was given to each servant, according to his abilities. In this parable, each servant received one mina, which evidently represents the spiritual equipment and the opportunities for service that are common to every servant of Christ. The truth that our Lord fits our responsibilities to our capacities is not in view here. All these servants are equal. The difference between the servant who made ten minas and the servant who made five minas would not therefore be a difference in ability or capacity; it is rather a difference in diligence and zeal.

In the parable of the sower the good seed brought forth fruit, thirty, sixty, and a hundredfold, and this shows that there are differences in fruit-bearing among Christians. It is also possible that a person with one special ability could be as faithful and zealous as someone with two or more special abilities, and these people would receive equal commendation and equal reward.

But in the parable of the minas the man who made good use of his mina and multiplied it ten times had a greater reward than the man who made five minas. This reward takes the shape of increased service and privilege and responsibility. One has the capacity to rule over ten cities, another the capacity to rule over five. This is not a matter of native gifts—for which one is not responsible—but rather the use of these gifts. The parable appeals to us to serve with zeal, earnestly seeking to win the highest reward possible.

In Christian service, it is not always the person with the greatest abilities who accomplishes the greatest results. Andrew won Peter, and so he has a share in all the fruit of Peter's life. The man who won D. L. Moody, and those who influenced his life, have a share in his fruit. Moreover, God is the one who gives the increase, and God could give increase from the work of very humble servants far greater than from the most gifted servants. Paul was one of the most gifted of all the servants of Christ, and he labored more abundantly than all the apostles. We may safely give him first place, among those whose deeds are recorded, for diligence and zeal in the service of the Lord.

The man who put the mina in a piece of cloth is sharply distinguished from those citizens who hated their master and did not want him to reign over them. The unfaithful servant does not lose sight of the fact that he is a servant. He represents the professing Christian who calls Jesus Christ Lord. This servant would not have the excuse that the man with the one talent had—that others had a greater amount entrusted to them. He received the same as the others, and this parable illustrates that, from one standpoint, all Christ's servants have an equal opportunity to win rewards. It is not said that this man is cast into outer darkness, but he does lose the mina.

Here again it is emphasized that the king was not interested in money. He was interested in the servant. He was in fact the opposite of the master described by this servant. Our Lord is not austere, reaping where He has not sown. He is the gracious Lord who has given Himself for us and who has suffered far more than any of His servants are called upon to suffer. Had this servant been faithful in working with the master's money, he would have possessed this, as well as all the increase. He remains a servant, though reprimanded by his master and losing his reward. Yet he is not classed with the wicked citizens who are destroyed.

Here again this parable is not given to tell us whether this servant is saved or lost. It is warning us against unfaithfulness. From other Scriptures, and from the experience of Christians, we can judge that this servant represents professing Christians, some of whom have never been born again, and others who may be saved after their faith is purified.

The citizens who would not have Christ reign over them vividly remind us of our Lord's own people Israel who answered, "We have no king but Caesar" (John 19:15). The destruction of Jerusalem and the scattering of Israel was a temporary, physical punishment for this rejection and crucifixion and also for the rejection of the risen, glorified Lord when He was proclaimed by Paul and the other apostles.

These citizens represent all those who refuse to have Christ as Savior and Lord. When He comes in glory Christ will reward His saints and punish those who reject Him. These two things are constantly linked in the prophetic Scriptures. And when Paul spoke to the Thessalonians who were suffering for Christ's sake, he said:

> God is just; He will pay back trouble to those who trouble you and give relief to you who are troubled, and to us as well. This will happen when the Lord Jesus is revealed from heaven in blazing fire with his powerful angels. He will punish those who do not know God and do not obey the gospel of our Lord Jesus. They will be punished with ever-lasting destruction and shut out from the presence of the Lord and from the majesty of his power on the day he comes to be glorified in his holy people and to be marveled at among all those who have believed. This includes you, because you believed our testimony to you. (2 Thess. 1:6-10)

This wonderful prophecy, we judge, refers to the coming of the Lord Jesus at the beginning of the millennial period. But this whole period of a thousand years is the Lord's day, His day of glory and of judgment, with climactic events at the beginning and at the end.

The parables, in presenting the truths of service, need not distinguish between these various events. The outstanding fact is that both the glory and the loss of these events are beyond all human comprehension.

THE FOUR PARABLES OF SERVICE

In lessons 7–10 we have studied four parables of service. When we bring these four parables together, we discover that the central spiritual messages are related to each other.

We have seen in the parable of the unworthy servant the foundation truth that we begin our service as those who have received Christ with all His riches, having been purchased by His precious blood. In Christian service, therefore, we can never do more than it is our duty to do, nor can we do anything that will repay our Lord for what He has done for us. Nevertheless, He does reward us for our service, as is indicated in the parable of the workers in the vineyard. The message of that parable is that we should not have the spirit of asking—"What's in it for me?"—but we are to serve, whether our service is short or long, with perfect confidence in the Lord who will graciously give us far more than we deserve or expect. The parable of the talents teaches that one of the principles on which rewards are given is: equal rewards for equal faithfulness in service, and unspeakable loss for unfaithfulness. Finally, we have the truth in the parable of the ten minas that there are different rewards for different degrees of zeal among those who are faithful servants.

There are two glorious facts concerning Christian service that run through these four parables. The first is that we serve a Person. When we speak of "church work" or "Christian service," there is a danger that we may forget the Person who is the foundation of all our service. What a difference if we can say that what we are doing is being done for the Lord Himself. One day we will enter into the joy of our Lord. Already now we may enter into the joy of serving Him, never counting the cost and never seeking merely to please others.

The second great fact, closely linked with the first, is the vital relation of Christian service to the return of our Lord. To be ready for His coming means to be faithful in doing the things He gives us to do. At the forefront of those who eagerly await the coming of the Lord are those who are zealous in evangelism and in missionary service.

Yet there is a danger that our interest in the signs of the times and our belief that the coming of the Lord is drawing near will detract from our zeal in taking the gospel to the ends of the earth (Acts 1:7-8). It is right that we should study the signs of the times. It is right that we should look up with expectation when we see things that were prophesied taking place. But we cannot say whether it will be ten years or a hundred years before our Lord returns. If we wish to be truly ready for Him, then all our Christian service should be done with this in mind. We are to do His work until He comes. We are not told to work until we think the coming is near at hand.

Unless we understand our Lord's plan, we will waste much effort because we will have a wrong view of what He expects us to accomplish in the present age. It is not God's purpose that the world be converted in this present age. The parable of the wheat and the tares indicates that righteousness and wickedness will continue in conflict until the very end of the age, when our Lord returns. Our part is to preach the gospel and to win souls, counting on His supernatural working in this task, but not expecting the present world system to be transformed into the kingdom of God.

REVIEW OF LESSON 10

1. What does this parable teach us concerning the establishment of the kingdom of God on earth?

2. What is the connection between our present service and this future kingdom of God?

3. How does the fact that each servant had one mina relate to the equality of all Christians? Does this have anything to do with salvation or service?

4. State in your own words the central teaching of this parable and the various related truths.

5. What shows that this parable was true to the conditions of that day?

PART V

PARABLES
OF
PRAYER

PREPARATION FOR LESSON 11

Reading Lesson: Luke 10:38–11:13

1. What is the occasion of this parable?
2. Does the incident in Luke 10:38-42 teach us anything about the right approach in prayer? (See also Phil. 4:6-7.)
3. What does our Lord say the spiritual message of this parable is? Sum up in your own words this central teaching.
4. Whom does the traveler in this story represent?
5. What additional teaching on prayer is given in Luke 11:11-13?

Lesson 11

The Friend at Midnight

Luke 11:5-8

There are two parables of our Lord that have teachings concerning prayer as their central message. There are in addition parable-similes (short parables) and parabolic sayings that give teaching on prayer, such as the son asking for bread and receiving a stone (Matt. 7:9). Both of the prayer parables are in Luke: the friend at midnight in chapter 11 and the judge and the persistent widow in chapter 18.

Many consider the parable of the Pharisee and the tax collector in Luke 18 a parable on prayer, but it was given to those who believed that they were righteous in themselves. It was given so that they could learn what true righteousness is. We have studied it as a parable of the Christian's heart. It tells of the way two men prayed, and so it does give a message concerning prayer. But the prayers of these men are given to contrast a right and wrong attitude toward God. It is teaching that we should come to God as humble and contrite sinners. This could have been taught by means of an illustration other than that of prayer.

Luke is the Gospel that sets forth the humanness of our Lord. All four Gospels reveal this aspect of Christ, just as each

141

of them presents every essential fact concerning Him. But Luke, the Gospel of the Son of Man and the universal Gospel, lays special emphasis on the prayer life of our Lord. It is Luke who tells us that our Lord was praying when the Holy Spirit descended at His baptism (3:21), that He spent all night in prayer before He selected His apostles (6:12), that He had been praying just prior to Peter's great confession (9:18), and that He was transfigured before Peter, James, and John "as he was praying" (9:29). It is fitting, then, that these two parables on prayer should be recorded by Luke.

The Setting (Luke 10:38–11:4)

"Lord, teach us to pray." This request is the occasion of both this parable (11:5-8) and of our Lord's repetition of the prayer He had given earlier in His Sermon on the Mount (11:2-4; Matt. 6:9-13). One of the disciples made this request after Jesus had finished praying; His example stirred in their hearts the desire to know how to pray.

In the Gospel of Luke this request follows the beautiful incident of Mary sitting at the feet of her Lord, listening to the words of Jesus. This scene is recorded only by Luke, and it may be taken as part of the setting of the parable of the friend at midnight, though it is not the occasion of it nor does it occur at the same time.

Mary is an example of someone who has the right attitude in prayer. She is carrying out the command of Philippians 4:6: "Do not be anxious about anything." Martha, her sister, is troubled about many things, but Mary has found the one thing necessary in life—quiet trust in the all-sufficient Savior and Lord.

We can learn something about the right approach to prayer from our Lord's answer to Martha. We should seek to pray with a quiet spirit and with a deep trust in God's care for us. When the disciples asked Him to teach them to pray, He answered by gathering all the principles of prayer into those few sentences that we call the Lord's Prayer. It is proper that we call this the Lord's Prayer, because it was Jesus who spoke these words. But in another sense we could call this the disciples' prayer, just as we could call the prayer in John 17 the Lord's Prayer. In any case, the Lord's Prayer, as given here, is part of the setting for the parable of the friend at midnight.

It is not our purpose here to study the marvelous teachings in this prayer, but we should take note that Jesus gave it in order to teach the disciples how to pray. And so it is much more than just a model prayer. It contains principles that should govern all of our prayer. This does not mean it is wrong to use it as a prayer; in fact, it is probably inevitable that Christians use these precious words as a prayer. We do need to guard against the danger of rigid forms of prayer and worship, namely the danger of this becoming mere formalism, which is an abomination to God.

Prayer should begin with the element of worship. So we pray, "Our Father which art in heaven, hallowed be thy name. Thy kingdom come. Thy will be done" (Matt. 6:9-10 KJV). We tend to rush into God's presence filled with our problems and needs and sins. But our hearts should first of all be occupied with coming into the presence of the holy God; we should be invoking His name and seeking His kingdom and His will.

Then comes the "daily bread" that satisfies our need for physical and spiritual nourishment, forgiveness of our sins, and victory over temptation. A friend of mine once said that as a child he used to pray, "Forgive us our sins as we ought to forgive those who sin against us." These words capture an important truth: Christians cannot truly repent of their sins if they withhold forgiveness from others. It is not that our forgiving others earns us forgiveness from God, nor is it that our forgiving others is the same as His forgiving us. But to the merciful, God can show mercy. Then by His grace we can forgive others, remembering the teaching of the parable of the unmerciful servant: What others owe us is a pittance in comparison to our debt to the Lord—like $2500 is to $825 million.

And when we pray "Lead us not into temptation," we are carrying out our Lord's injunction to "watch and pray so that you will not fall into temptation" (Mark 14:38). That is, we must pray that we do not enter into temptation, which leads to sin.

After giving this prayer, our Lord tells the parable of the friend at midnight. It is an important part of the answer to the request, "Lord, teach us to pray."

The Story (Luke 11:5-8)

A friend coming at midnight needing food for an unexpected guest is a situation that would be quite familiar to our Lord's hearers. There were few public accommodations for travelers in that time, and the emphasis on hospitality in Jewish culture made it incumbent on this man to take his friend in. He had nothing to set before his guest; so he went to another friend's house to ask for three loaves of bread.

In verse 7 we read that this family was sleeping in one bed; so it is quite natural that the husband did not want to rise and possibly awaken his entire family. However, the man outside explained why he needed the bread; he was not asking frivolously. Evidently he kept asking and would not go away until his friend gave him what he wanted.

The fact that the man outside was a friend did not cause the husband to get out of bed. But when it became evident that the only way to satisfy this friend would be to give him what he wanted, he rose and gave him three loaves of bread. He knew his family would be wakened whether he got out of bed or not, and he also knew he would have rest for neither mind nor body if he did not satisfy this request.

So the story is a simple one; but it is a vivid illustration yet today, and it was certainly true to the life of that time.

The Spiritual Message (Luke 11:9-10)

Our Lord Himself gives the message of this parable in a series of proverbs or parabolic sayings.

> So I say to you: Ask and it will be given to you; seek and you will find; knock and the door will be opened to you. For everyone who asks receives; he who seeks finds; and to him who knocks, the door will be opened.

We may sum up the central truth of this parable by saying: There is no such thing as unanswered prayer; we are to keep on praying until we get the answer. In commanding us to "ask . . . seek . . . knock," Christ is using a figure of speech. This is true in every part of life: Those who ask, receive; those who seek, find; and for those who knock, it is opened. James sums up this truth in his terse style when he says: "You do not have, because you do not ask God" (James 4:2).

Our Lord gives this truth in a more positive form; He tells us that every prayer will be answered if we keep on praying until the answer comes. He realized that we are often tempted to stop praying. After all other conditions are met, we need to persist in prayer until the answer comes.

We should focus our attention on the persistence of the man who asked for the three loaves. His friend's unwillingness to accommodate him is an understandable reaction, but in no way does this represent God. He is not reluctant to give; He is far more willing to give than we are to ask. In fact, this part of the parable suggests a contrast to God. If friends will at last give in to our persistent requests, how much more will God answer His children who continue to call on Him in prayer.

In this parable the request is soon granted, but we should not conclude from this that all our prayers will be answered speedily. Answers to prayer may be delayed for various reasons. We may be asking for the wrong thing or asking with a wrong motive. Or it could be that our request is entirely in accordance with His will, but there are spiritual forces to be overcome before the answer can be given.

We read that Daniel's words were heard, but one of the host of evil angels delayed the coming of God's messenger twenty-one days (Dan. 10:12-13). And when God was bringing the children of Israel into Canaan, four hundred years passed because the iniquity of the Amorites was not full (Gen. 15:13-16). God uses our prayers as part of the spiritual forces that overcome the devil's evil designs. Whenever God does delay in answering, it is for our good and the good of others. Here also we find that all things are working together for good to those who love God.

The traveler who came at midnight represents all those who are needy and come to us, especially those who need the Bread of Life. We have nothing of our own to give them. We must go to our all-sufficient Friend and ask of Him. How striking it is that in the picture of prayer presented here, the one who is praying does not ask about personal needs, he prays for the welfare of another. Someone has named these three men the needy friend, the praying friend, and the Mighty Friend. The man who asks for three loaves of bread represents the Christian. The request for *three* loaves suggests that we should be specific when we pray.

A missionary was leading a prayer meeting in a church in which the people were being asked to help send a young man to the mission field. The missionary interrupted their prayers to ask: "Why are you folks praying in such a general way? How much money do we need?"

Someone answered, "Five hundred dollars."

"Then let's ask God to send five hundred dollars for this young man to go to the mission field," the missionary said.

The prayers became very specific from that point on.

After the meeting one of the people told him, "Three hundred seventy-five dollars has already been given, and the rest has been promised!"

Everything in the parable of the friend at midnight points us to the central truth: We must be persistent in prayer. Keep on praying until the answer comes.

And there is no such thing as unanswered prayer. This is not to say that God grants all our requests; we should rejoice that He does not. But when He lets us know that our prayer is not in accordance with His will, or tells us to pray about a different matter, or lovingly refuses the request and asks us to trust Him, then our prayer is answered.

"Lord, teach us to pray." In answer to this request, our Lord taught His disciples how to pray and what to pray. And in the parable of the friend at midnight He added the instruction that we so often forget: *Pray*.

The Added Parable-Similes (Luke 11:11-13)

After explaining this parable, our Lord adds, "Which of you fathers, if your son asks for a fish, will give him a snake instead? Or if he asks for an egg, will give him a scorpion?" This added illustration is what we call a parable-simile.

The teaching here goes beyond our persistence and the graciousness of God to the fact that God gives us not only what we ask for but also something infinitely greater. In Matthew 7:11 our Lord follows up this parable-simile with these words: "How much more will your Father in heaven give good gifts to those who ask him?" In Luke the parallel passage reads as follows: "How much more will your Father in heaven give the Holy Spirit to those who ask him?" These two verses are not saying different things; each reveals the marvelous truth that it is through the Holy Spirit that we receive every spiritual gift, including the lesser material gifts.

Our Lord told His disciples, "All that belongs to the Father is mine" (John 16:15). And this same truth is stated in John 3:35: "The Father loves the Son and has placed everything in his hands." When Jesus was on earth, God gave everything into His hand by giving Him the Holy Spirit (John 3:34).

Now that Christ has ascended, the Holy Spirit takes the things of Christ and reveals them to us. God has given all things to our Lord. He also gives Christ to us; and both the Father and the Son send the Holy Spirit, and He takes the things of Christ and reveals them to us (John 16:14). So it is that when we pray we can receive all the riches of God's grace.

Since the Holy Spirit has been given and since He dwells within every Christian, the question naturally arises whether we should pray for the Holy Spirit. Many say that this is what Christ is telling us in Luke 11:13, but it may be better to interpret this passage as referring to the fact that the riches of God's grace, which are given to us by means of the Holy Spirit, come to us through the avenue of prayer. When we pray for the Holy Spirit, we are not thereby saying that He is not already present in our hearts. We are praying for the gifts and the miracles that are wrought by the Holy Spirit. It is in this sense that the Father gives us good gifts and the Holy Spirit.

REVIEW OF LESSON 11

1. What principles of prayer are given in the Lord's Prayer?

2. Should today's Christian use this prayer?

3. In what sense does God answer every true prayer?

4. What are some reasons he sometimes delays in answering?

5. Does this parable teach that God is ever reluctant or unwilling to answer our prayers?

PREPARATION FOR LESSON 12

Reading Lesson: Luke 17:20–18:8

1. What is the setting of this parable?
2. In your opinion, does the unjust judge represent God?
3. What does the passage preceding this parable teach concerning the Lord's return?
4. What does the passage following this parable teach concerning His return?
5. What is the central message of this parable?

Lesson 12

The Persistent Widow

Luke 18:2-5

Although the stories in the parable of the friend at midnight and the parable of the persistent widow differ considerably, both of these accounts press home the same message: We should be persistent in prayer. In one case a man asks a friend for food for an unexpected guest, and in the other parable a woman asks a judge for justice against an adversary. There are a number of such cases in Scripture in which our Lord sets forth the same spiritual message on different occasions.

We find that when a parable does present the same central truth as an earlier parable, it provides a richer, fuller unfolding of this truth or it offers some additional spiritual food. The parable of the persistent widow fits into the first category. Jesus here exhorts us to persist in our prayers for deliverance from suffering and affliction. The setting shows that this parable is applying the need for persistence in prayer to this area of Christian experience.

The Setting (Luke 17:20–18:1)

Luke provides the immediate setting of this parable: "Then Jesus told his disciples a parable to show them that they

151

should always pray and not give up." This statement is evidently closely connected with the discussion of the end of the age and the second coming in the preceding verses, because at the close of this parable Jesus again refers to His coming: "However, when the Son of Man comes, will he find faith on the earth?" (18:8). This indicates that this parable is part of His instruction concerning His personal return and the coming kingdom.

Jesus spoke this parable during His last journey to Jerusalem, before He approached Jericho (Luke 18:31-35). As this journey was drawing to a close, while His disciples and the people following after Him were intensely interested in an earthly kingdom of God, the Pharisees asked Jesus when the kingdom of God would come (17:20). He answered: "The kingdom of God does not come visibly, nor will people say, 'Here it is,' or 'There it is,' because the kingdom of God is within you" (17:20-21). The last clause here may also be translated, "The kingdom of God is in the midst of you," and some understand this to mean that since He, the King, was in their midst, the kingdom of God was in that sense there. It is clear He did not mean to say that these Pharisees, many of whom hated Him and counted Him an enemy, had the kingdom of God dwelling within them. It would seem quite natural to take these words to mean that the kingdom of God is a matter of the heart, not a matter of looking here or there to see it coming, as the Pharisees were doing. They were looking for an outward kingdom that had nothing to do with a change of heart.

It is significant that after making this statement to the Pharisees, our Lord turned to His disciples and spoke to them concerning the day of the Son of Man. "For the Son of Man in his day will be like the lightning, which flashes and lights up the sky from one end to the other" (Luke 17:24). It is true that the kingdom of God is a matter of the heart, but this does not mean that the clear prophecies of the establishment of the kingdom of God on earth are not to be literally fulfilled. Christ tells the disciples that first, before the kingdom comes, He must suffer many things and be rejected, and then He goes on to prophesy that conditions at the time of His coming will be similar to the days of Noah and the days of Lot. Thus, as He draws near to His death and resurrection, He gives instructions concerning His second coming. We have already noted that as He was about to enter Jerusalem, they expected the kingdom of God immediately to appear, and He gave them the parable of the ten minas to correct this impression (19:11). Nothing could be clearer than Christ's teaching that the kingdom of God will appear and be established on earth when He returns the second time.

Jesus had taught His disciples that He would not establish His kingdom on earth for some time. In the parable of the talents He said that the master who went away came back "after a long time" (Matt. 25:19). And all the other parables concerning this period between His first and second comings, which is a time of the growing of weeds and wheat, suggest that it would be an extended period.

Our present age of proclaiming the gospel to all nations was an utterly new revelation to the disciples, and only very slowly did they come to understand it. They needed faith and courage as the hoped-for earthly kingdom was put forward to the future.

This, therefore, is what our Lord had in mind when He spoke a parable to them "that they should always pray and not give up" (Luke 18:1). His disciples would be in danger of giving up because His coming was delayed. They might become discouraged because of the difficulties of the way and because of the suffering they would experience. It is quite evident that this parable points to prayer as the great resource of Christ's church in the days before His second coming.

The Story (Luke 18:2-5)

The unjust judge, "who neither feared God nor cared about men," refused the widow's plea for justice. It is clear from the judge's words in verses 4 and 5 that her cause was a just one. It is not necessary for us to know how her adversary had oppressed her. Perhaps her property had been unjustly taken from her. Whatever the circumstances may have been, she came for justice, which this judge was well able to give. Many widows, at the first refusal by a rough, disdainful judge, would have gone away and nursed their sorrow. This widow kept coming again and again, and evidently it was in her mind to keep coming until her request was granted.

The judge finally concluded that though neither fear of God nor concern for others would cause him to do justice, yet because he was tired of having her come he would accede to her request. The expression "wear me out" is in the Greek literally "bruise," that is, to strike a blow, as with a club. Some have interpreted this literally, but the expression here is doubtless to be taken figuratively.

As with many parables, the story is brief; yet the picture is clear and vivid, true to life, and full of human interest.

The Spiritual Message (Luke 18:6-8)

The message of this parable is that if a widow can obtain justice by continually calling on an unrighteous judge, who fears not God nor regards man, how much more should Christians be encouraged to persist in their cries to the Judge of all the earth, who will do right. "And the Lord said, 'Listen to what the unjust judge says. And will not God bring about justice for his chosen ones, who cry out to him day and night? Will he keep putting them off?'" If the unjust judge avenged the widow, will not God avenge His elect, whom He loves with a great and tender love, who are so dear to Him that they are called "the apple of his eye" (Zech. 2:8)? All the cries of God's people through the ages are heard. "The cries of the harvesters have reached the ears of the Lord Almighty" (James 5:4).

All the sufferings and tribulations of God's people constitute a cry to Him for deliverance. Throughout the Scriptures, the day of wrath is prophesied, but its coming has been long delayed. When the church becomes rich and complacent, with no sense of need, and when God's people become conformed to this present age, then these words seem to have little relevance, for Christians are not crying out for deliverance. But we should expect to suffer and Paul's message to the Thessalonians is one of the many passages that treat the elements of affliction and deliverance found in this parable.

> Therefore, among God's churches we boast about your perseverance and faith in all the persecutions and trials you are enduring. All this is evidence that God's judgment is right, and as a result you will be counted worthy of the kingdom of God, for which you are suffering. God is just: He will pay back trouble to those who trouble you and give relief to you who are troubled, and to us as well. This will happen when the Lord Jesus is revealed from heaven in blazing fire with his powerful angels. He will punish those who do not know God and do not obey the gospel of our Lord Jesus. They will be punished with everlasting destruction and shut out from the presence of the Lord and from the majesty of his power on the day he comes to be glorified in his holy people and to be marveled at among all those who have believed. This includes you, because you believed our testimony to you. (2 Thess. 1:4-10)

This was written nineteen hundred years ago, and that day of wrath and judgment is still future. Nevertheless, these words apply in every age, for the day of vengeance is sure to come. Here, too, we find that what our Lord sums up in a few unforgettable sentences in a parable is expanded on by the writers of the Epistles.

God appears to be slow in giving justice, and this seems similar to the unrighteous judge refusing the plea of the widow. However, the judge's motive is entirely different from what is in the heart of God. The judge represents God by way of contrast. God is longsuffering with His saints because He loves them, and He knows that "our light and momentary troubles are achieving for us an eternal glory that far outweighs them all" (2 Cor. 4:17). Also, God loves those who do not love Him and desires that they should repent and turn to Him.

In answer to the question whether God will not avenge His elect who cry to Him for deliverance our Lord in most emphatic words answers, "I tell you, he will see that they get justice, and quickly." The word "quickly" has troubled many. If He has delayed for over nineteen centuries, can we call the deliverance quick? But it is very evident that both ideas are here, namely, a long delay and a speedy deliverance. The deliverance will be quick because God will not delay one moment beyond the necessary time. He Himself is most eager for that moment to come when there shall be no more delay and when He can wipe away every tear from the eyes of His children (Rev. 10:6). Meanwhile, that delay has worked out for many blessings to His people. We are to have a share in the glorious kingdom, and this would not have been had not His plan been delayed.

But there is another sense in which the word "quickly" is to be understood. While there is long delay in the working out of God's purposes, the consummation of them will come so suddenly and will be accomplished so speedily that it will illustrate the saying that one day with the Lord is as a thousand years (Rev. 22:20; 2 Peter 3:8-10).

Our Lord concludes this parable with a question: "However, when the Son of Man comes, will he find faith on the earth?" Or "will he find the faith on the earth?" He does not say that He will not find faith on the earth; He is asking a question. He has already made it very clear that there will be weeds and wheat until the very end and that at His coming He will catch up those who are His own. It would seem here that "the faith" refers to our expectation that Christ will come again at any time.

Before our Lord's first coming, only a small remnant were looking for Him. Nearly all of His chosen people had become weary in their expectation of the Messiah and were occupied with their own affairs, seeking satisfaction in the things of the world. In this parable our Lord tells His listeners that it will be like that at His second coming. The world will not be expecting Him. In modern times, in spite of all the teaching, true and false, concerning the personal return of Christ, the world as a whole and even many Christians regard such talk as fiction. Men are not looking for any such revelation from the heavens. Our Lord's question, however, is not so much prophetic as it is an exhortation that His own people should guard against failing faith and discouragement during the long delay of His coming and judging the wicked.

In our Lord's farewell discourse to His disciples on the Mount of Olives, He warned them: "Because of the increase of wickedness, the love of most will grow cold" (Matt. 24:12). This warning applies to every generation of Christians, though its final fulfillment will take place at the close of the age, before our Lord Jesus returns.

The Personal Application

This parable is relevant for every Christian in every age. We do not know when our Lord will come, and we should always be watching for Him. Christians throughout the ages are appointed to suffer, and in our personal sorrows, in the oppression and sorrow of the poor, and in the persecutions of God's people, we should remember that our God is mindful of every cry. Our part is always to pray and not faint.

In the parable of the friend at midnight, we have an appeal to persistence in all our prayer. In this parable we are urged to pray about our tribulations and difficulties, with the certainty that our cry will be answered, though there be long delay. In many individual cases, our prayers may seem to be unanswered. Loved ones will lose their lives. Terrible injustice will prevail. But we are certain that these things are but love's delays and the greater the tribulation, the greater will be the coming glory.

This parable does not mean that our Lord wants us always to be in anguish. He provides His own joy and blessing in this present age, and we are to learn how to abound as well as how to suffer need. But in the midst of our peace and joy, we are fellowshiping with the sufferings of Christ, and our hearts should go out for the sufferings of the whole world. When we find ourselves in pleasant circumstances and all of our needs are provided, we should have more leisure to enter into the needs and sufferings of others. When one member of the body of Christ suffers, all the members suffer. It may be that saints in various places are giving up their lives for Christ's sake. We should enter into their sorrows. The teachings of Satan are prevailing here and there throughout the church of Christ. We should take this as our own burden, even though this may not affect the immediate field in which we are working.

In proportion to the faithfulness of the church of Christ in glorifying her Lord, in that proportion will the enemy fight against her; and in this way the persecutions and tribulations of the early church will be reenacted. Particularly as the age draws to a close, will this be more and more true. Christ's own people will be separated unto Him and then His exhortation that we "should always pray and not give up" will be especially needed.

REVIEW OF LESSON 12

1. In what respect does the spiritual message of this parable go beyond that of the parable of the friend at midnight?

2. What does this parable teach about the second coming of Christ?

3. What does this parable teach about what it will be like for Christians prior to His appearance?

4. In what way are Christians to be avenged?

5. Why, do you think, does God delay His deliverance of His people?

PART VI

PARABLES
OF
STEWARDSHIP

PREPARATION FOR LESSON 13

Reading Lesson: Luke 12:13-48. Read also Luke 11:37–12:12.

1. What was the occasion of our Lord telling this parable?
2. Should we conclude that this rich man was dishonest?
3. What does Leviticus 25:23 teach concerning the owner-ship of money and property?
4. What is the central truth of this parable?
5. What is the chief reason this rich man is called a "fool"?

Lesson 13

The Rich Fool

Luke 12:16-20

Money is a test of character. Most men slip and fall in the face of this test. Our Lord's teaching on money and its use is as practical for the twentieth century as it was in the first century. Are we Christians applying this teaching?

In three of our Lord's parables there is particular reference to the stewardship of money, and we have called these parables of stewardship. It should be carefully noted in the beginning, however, that stewardship applies not only to money but to time and to all of life's activities. In this sense every parable is a parable of stewardship. It is also true that money, standing for all material possessions, is a vital test of how we are living. Money can be thought of as representing our labor here on earth and all that we spend or invest. Thus our Lord's teachings on money apply to the whole stewardship of life.

We begin with the study of the rich fool, a parable that was occasioned, as so many our Lord's teachings were, by an interruption.

The Setting (Luke 12:13-15)

During His last journey to Jerusalem our Lord came into

conflict with the Pharisees and denounced them. He turned from this to give comfort to the disciples, reminding them that the "very hairs of your head are all numbered" (12:7). He goes on to repeat His warning against the unpardonable sin of blasphemy against the Holy Spirit.

In the midst of these solemn teachings concerning the great conflict that is to come between His disciples and His enemies, a man from the multitude that was following after Jesus cried out, "Teacher, tell my brother to divide the inheritance with me." Here we have a little glimpse of the way in which the people regarded the Lord Jesus. We may suppose that this man was honest and that his brother was really seeking unjustly to take his share of an inheritance. He recognized Christ as a just arbitrator. Perhaps he and his brother were both disciples of the Lord. In any case, we see a man concerned with his own affairs—concerned that he might be defrauded.

In His usual startling way, Christ meets this demand directly and then gives a teaching that goes to the heart of the issue. First, He asks: "Man, who appointed me a judge or an arbiter between you?" This question sets forth the great principle that Christ did not come to settle disputes of this sort. He came to enunciate the principles by which men should themselves judge and decide. This does not mean that Christ is indifferent to justice. It means that His work was not to enter into the application of justice in specific instances.

The principle has important applications, including the truth that God leaves a great deal to men, allowing them to arrange their government affairs, their business affairs, and their family affairs according to their own judgment, using the great principles of righteousness that God's law sets forth. From a practical standpoint, we can understand how crippling it would have been for the Lord to step aside from His appointed ministry to judge concerning material things.

But going deeper than this request for Him to judge, the

Lord makes the question an occasion for vital teaching concerning "greed." This man's brother may have unjustly taken his inheritance, but this injustice was the occasion of revealing the greed of his own heart. Our Lord said to all of them, "Watch out! Be on your guard against all kinds of greed; a man's life does not consist in the abundance of his possessions."

The parable of the rich fool illustrates this searching truth, which is so contrary to all of their conceptions and especially contrary to the views of the Pharisees who were at that time pressing in on Him. They were lovers of money, and they judged that a man's life and standing consisted in the abundance of the things he possessed. Yet consider Christ Himself! He had richness and fullness of life, but He possessed practically nothing.

The Story (Luke 12:16-20)

A rich man, increasing in riches and planning to pile them up for the years to come, is the picture given in the parable. He was the owner of large farms, which brought forth plentifully. His barns were already filled, and he had no place to lay up the large and perhaps unexpected increase. He could have given away the grain.

We might ask why he did not sell the grain, but in those days grain was frequently laid up in storehouses as a valuable and permanent form of wealth. He decided to pull down his barns and build greater ones, and he did this with a self-centered purpose, saying to himself, "You have plenty of good things laid up for many years. Take life easy; eat, drink and be merry."

There is nothing in this story of ill-gotten wealth. The man was honest, and his increase came as a result of his own sowing and reaping. There is no suggestion here that he did not pay his laborers well. Nor is there any suggestion that this

man was wicked or given to riotous living. When he says;
"Take life easy; eat, drink and be merry," he is not necessarily
thinking of a life of evil indulgence. His sin is not dishonesty,
nor wickedness, nor drunkenness.

But God said to him, "You fool! This very night your life
will be demanded from you. Then who will get what you have
prepared for yourself?" This is part of the parable story, God's
message coming to the man on the same night that he rea-
soned concerning the goods that he had laid up for many
years. What a searching question that is, "Who will get what
you have prepared for yourself?"

The Spiritual Message (Luke 12:21)

Our Lord gives the meaning of this parable in one of His
unforgettable sentences: "This is how it will be with anyone
who stores up things for himself but is not rich toward God."
The two uses of money are here set forth—laying it up for
ourselves and using it for the glory of God.

There follows a discourse to the disciples concerning trusting in God to supply all of their needs. He tells them to "consider the ravens" and "consider . . . the lilies" (vv. 24, 27). He
tells them not to be concerned about their food and clothing,
for the Father knows their need of these things. He repeats the
message of the Sermon on the Mount, namely to seek first the
kingdom of God and to trust God to add all needed material
things.

Then He gives them that precious double metaphor: "Do
not be afraid, little flock, for your Father has been pleased to
give you the kingdom" (v. 32). What a contrast there is between a little flock of sheep and the kingdom they are to
receive, the contrast between their present poverty and their
future wealth. In view of this, He tells them, "Sell your possessions and give to the poor. Provide purses for yourselves
that will not wear out, a treasure in heaven that will not be

exhausted, where no thief comes near and no moth destroys. For where your treasure is, there your heart will be also" (vv. 33-34).

Our Lord goes on with the exhortation to be ever waiting for His coming, to be faithful as servants waiting for their master. He adds the parable of the faithful and wicked servants, the parable of the thief breaking through, the parable of the wise steward and the wicked steward, unfaithful in his master's absence.

All of these may be used as part of our Lord's explanation of the message of the parable and as illustrations of His command to take heed and keep ourselves from all greed. But let's search out the application of the parable of the rich fool.

The Personal Application

In our day the expression "a rich fool" is a very unusual one. We do not think of rich people as being foolish. We often speak of "a poor fool." We use the proverb "A fool and his money are soon parted" to refer to the fact that one who does not have good sense may easily be separated from his money. But this rich man was not that kind of a fool. He was one who was not to be parted from his money, at least according to his own planning. He was making careful provision to keep his increasing riches. But God called him a fool, literally one who was without mind or without good sense, having no sound principles on which to base his judgment.

The reason this man was a fool is because he believed his wealth was his own. The fundamental teaching concerning money and material things throughout the Bible is that man is a steward. That is, he does not own a single dollar or a single foot of ground. Men are accustomed to think of this as a figurative statement or a teaching of ministers who use it as an appeal for money, but this is literal truth.

When God asked, "Who will get what you have prepared

for yourself?" He was striking at the root error of this rich man, who believed that his wealth was his own and that it was his to do with as he pleased. His sudden death, leaving behind all that he had laid up, shows that those material things were simply a temporary stewardship. His life did not consist in the abundance of the things he possessed. When God required his soul, or his life, he went out naked, as it were, into the presence of God.

When God gave Canaan to His chosen people, He gave them laws for the ordering of land. Among them was this: "The land must not be sold permanently, because the land is mine and you are but aliens and my tenants" (Lev. 25:23). All the earth belongs to God, and men are sojourners and pilgrims here. God's own people acknowledge that they are sojourners and pilgrims on the earth, though they do not always act accordingly. No person, Christian or non-Christian, possesses a single foot of land. The land is God's and all material wealth is His. When man handles it as though it were his own, then his folly is evident.

> For all can see that wise men die; the foolish and the senseless alike perish and leave their wealth to others. Their tombs will remain their houses forever, their dwellings for endless generations, though they had named lands after themselves. But man, despite his riches, does not endure; he is like the beasts that perish. This is the fate of those who trust in themselves, and of their followers, who approve their sayings. (Ps. 49:10-13)

The Psalmist thus presses home the folly of trusting in riches and gives the same message that our Lord here puts into this striking parable. The Psalmist continues,

> Do not be overawed when a man grows rich, when the splendor of his house increases; for he will take nothing with him when he dies, his splendor will not descend with him. Though while he lived he counted himself blessed—and

men praise you when you prosper—he will join the generation of his fathers, who will never see the light of life. A man who has riches without understanding is like the beasts that perish. (Ps. 49:16-20)

That is, men are fools when they think that their earthly possessions belong to them. Yet all generations keep on applauding them and calling them wise, though God calls them fools.

Likewise in Psalm 39 the vanity of life is set forth: "He heaps up wealth, not knowing who will get it" (Ps. 39:6). The wise man answers this question as to who will get it by revealing that "a sinner's wealth is stored up for the righteous" (Prov. 13:22), that the unjust man gathers wealth "for another, who will be kind to the poor" (Prov. 28:8; cf. Job 27:15, 17). The sinner gathers and heaps up "to hand it over to the one who pleases God" (Eccl. 2:26).

In the other parables of stewardship, we will see this same message of man as a steward pressed home. The parable of the rich fool teaches that since man is a steward he should never lay up treasure for himself but should be rich toward God. Money is for but one purpose—to give away or invest in eternal things.

We need not suppose that our Lord was speaking primarily of a literal action when He said, "Sell your possessions and give to the poor. Provide purses for yourselves that will not wear out, a treasure in heaven that will not be exhausted, where no thief comes near and no moth destroys. For where your treasure is, there your heart will be also" (Luke 12:33-34). He was laying down the great principle that earthly wealth should be used for laying up eternal treasure. A businessman cannot sell all that he has and give alms, for then he could not carry on his business. It is not that a man should give away all his wealth, but that he should recognize the principle that his money is to be used for God.

This applies, however, not only to wealthy men but to all

who have money in any degree. When writing to the Ephesians about practical everyday living, Paul commanded, "He
who has been stealing must steal no longer, but must work,
doing something useful with his own hands, that he may have
something to share with those in need" (Eph. 4:28). Here we
have an incidental expression of what is considered a fundamental Christian principle—that the reason for laboring and
making money is to give that money away, not to lay it up for
ourselves. What a terrible indictment of the way we handle
money and our attitude in the use of our riches! Do we not use
money as though it belonged to us, after giving a tenth or some
other portion to the Lord for His service?

The rich man sought to satisfy his soul with material things.
In this also he was foolish, but the central thought of the
parable is his greed, his judgment that material riches constitute the real riches.

Greed is listed among the terrible sins and is called idolatry.
Idolatry is the worship of false gods, or the putting of some
person or some thing in the place of God. Greed is idolatry
because our love is set on material things instead of on God.
The cure for greed, therefore, is a single-hearted love for God,
a passion for the kingdom of God, a living for the unseen
world.

The wise man seeks souls. He is a lover of men. The foolish
man seeks money. He is a lover of mammon.

REVIEW OF LESSON 13

1. Why did Christ refuse to decide the case of the man who wanted part of the inheritance?

2. In what ways was the rich man righteous?

3. In what ways was he an unfaithful steward?

4. How does our Lord apply the truth of this parable?

5. How does this apply to poor people as well as to the rich?

PREPARATION FOR LESSON 14

Reading Lesson: Luke 16:1-18

1. To whom was this parable spoken?
2. What other listeners heard it?
3. Who commended the shrewd manager? For what was he commended?
4. Why did this manager reduce the debts of his lord's debtors?
5. What is the central truth of this parable?

Lesson 14

The Shrewd Manager

Luke 16:1-8

All parables help to draw aside the veil between the unseen world and this present material world. But there is one parable in particular that draws a remarkable parallel between the material things of this life and the eternal things of the unseen world. The parable of the shrewd manager, often referred to as the parable of the unrighteous steward, deals with the stewardhip of money, and it also gives principles that affect the whole stewardship of life.

The parable has attracted special interest because of the commendation of the shrewd manager. But there need be no difficulty about the interpretation of the parable, if the right principles are followed. It is the story of a dishonest or unrighteous manager, but it will be seen that the more accurate title of the parable is the shrewd manager.

The Setting (Luke 16:1)

The only introduction to this parable is the opening clause in Luke 16:1, "Jesus told his disciples." These words immediately follow the parable of the lost son in Luke 15. They indicate that the parable of the shrewd manager was spoken to

173

the disciples, as well as to the tax collectors and sinners who were following Him, and it was spoken in the presence of the scribes and Pharisees who murmured at His receiving sinners. In answer to their murmuring, He had given the parables of the lost sheep, the lost coin, and the lost son. These parables revealed the love of the Father's heart and His yearning for lost men. This love was quite in contrast with the attitude of the hard-hearted Pharisees.

After our Lord told the parable of the shrewd manager, we read the following: "The Pharisees, who loved money, heard all this and were sneering at Jesus" (Luke 16:14). These Pharisees were not lovers of men; they were lovers of money. This makes it evident that the teaching was very much needed, not only to instruct the disciples but also to reveal the wrong attitude toward God and toward life that was in the hearts of these religious leaders.

Some have understood that the Lord, in giving this parable, had especially in mind the tax collectors who were coming to accept Him as Savior and who needed to be taught about the righteous handling of money. However, it will be seen that the teaching goes much deeper than the honest or dishonest use of money. This parable presents principles that should govern the Christian's attitude toward eternal things.

The Story (Luke 16:1-8)

The manager, as was common in those days, had complete charge of his master's goods, in somewhat the same way that Joseph had charge of all of Potiphar's household. Word came to the master that this manager was wasting these goods; that is, he was unfaithful. Apparently he used money freely both for his own pleasure and for that of his friends. The master told him he was to be dismissed, and he was to get his books into shape promptly.

Perhaps he had but a few days, but during those days he

was still in charge of his master's goods. He began to think about the future. He knew that he had no strength to do ordinary labor, and he did not want to become an object of charity. Soon he had a brilliant idea. He went to his master's debtors, perhaps to all of them, and used his authority as manager to reduce their obligations. These people were probably tenants who paid for their rent and their seed from what they produced.

The parable tells of two of these debtors. The debt of the man who owed eight hundred gallons of oil was changed to four hundred gallons. Four hundred gallons of olive oil would perhaps be the equivalent of three hundred days' labor, though it is very difficult to be sure about the value of products in those days. The second man owed a thousand bushels of wheat. The reduction of his debt by two hundred bushels was the equivalent of about four hundred days' labor.

The master heard what had been done, and his statement has caused difficulty for many: "The master commended the dishonest manager because he had acted shrewdly." The King James Version reads, "And the lord." Some have mistakenly supposed that this refers to the Lord Jesus. The statement is part of the story and refers, of course, to the master.

It should also be noted that the master did not commend him for his unrighteousness but because he had acted shrewdly. The master recognized his prudence and foresight, but he was not making any comment on the morality of the transaction. He admired the cleverness of the manager's trick, and since it was all over and he could do nothing to change it, he took the matter, we might say, as "a good sport."

The Spiritual Message (Luke 16:8-18)

Many students have regarded this parable as a teaching on the unrighteousness of the manager and a warning to Christians that they should not imitate him. He *was* an unfaithful manager and was losing his position on that account. This certainly is not an example that Christians should follow.

When he was told of his dismissal, he adopted a dishonest method of dealing with his master's debtors. This, again, is something that Christians should not imitate. But neither the unfaithfulness of the manager nor his dishonesty is the central feature of the story. It is the shrewdness of the manager in feathering his own nest that is the central point. Likewise, this forms the central spiritual message. Christians are, in the spiritual realm, to imitate this prudence in the material realm.

In the interpretation of this parable, therefore, we see the vital importance of the three principles that must be observed when seeking the spiritual meaning of a parable: (1) there is one central message; (2) there are several details of the parable that have spiritual significance but all center in the one truth; and (3) there are details belonging to the story that are not intended to have spiritual significance. In this parable the fact that the manager is unrighteous is an important and necessary part of the story; it lends vividness to it. But this item is not intended to give a special spiritual message. Some might draw two lessons from the parable—to avoid the unrighteousness of the manager and to imitate his shrewdness. But the purpose of this parable is to press home one central truth, not two.

The spiritual message of the parable is given very clearly by our Lord as He draws a series of great parallels. First, He challenges Christians by the example of this unrighteous manager who shows such prudence in the things of the world: "For the people of this world are more shrewd in dealing with their own kind than are the people of the light." The people of this world are those who live as though this were the only age. What they do here has no reference to any other world or to any other time except the future of their earthly life here. All unsaved men are "people of this world." But it is doubtless true that there are many professing Christians, and also some real Christians, who live as "people of this world," handling money and material things as though their real life were here.

The "people of the light" refers to Christians, the children of God, who have the light of life and who should not walk in darkness but should understand the real meaning of life. Our Lord does not say that the people of this world are wiser than the people of the light. He says that "with their own kind" they are more shrewd than the people of the light are in relation to spiritual things. This does not mean that all the people of the light are in this condemnation; indeed, the parable is given for the purpose of having Christians learn the secret of true stewardship.

The people of the world show more sense in material things than Christians show in spiritual things. This person in the parable, who was handling earthly things, showed real prudence in providing for his earthly future while the people of the light, Christian believers, show very little prudence in providing for eternity. The teaching on how to be spiritually wise is given in a series of remarkable lessons drawn from this parable by our Lord.

1. *Christians are stewards.* As the man in the story possessed not one dollar of his own but handled his master's money, so the money and other material things that we are handling do not belong to us. We are handling God's property. This truth was clearly brought out in the parable of the rich fool studied in the preceding lesson.

2. *This stewardship of ours is temporary.* It will come to an end, just as the stewardship of the man in the story came to an end. Our stewardship will end either at death or at the coming of the Lord Jesus Christ. From now until then we have control of these material things entrusted to us, just as the manager had control of his master's money.

3. *The money and material things that we handle here are shadows.*

The riches of the unseen world are real. This is the meaning of our Lord's statement in contrasting "worldly wealth" with "true riches" in verse 11. The word "true" has the sense of "real," as contrasted with that which is shadow. In the same sense, our Lord is called "the true bread" and "the true vine" (John 6:32; 15:11). Money is called "worldly wealth," not because it is evil in itself, but because this present world is evil and money is not handled according to God's plan.

Christians living in the world need to handle material things, but money for the most part is the instrument of those who are not living for God but for this present life. We must choose between God and money. When we choose money, it becomes a god to us. The Scriptures seem to condemn riches in an unqualified way in several instances. This is not because it is evil in itself to be rich but because nearly all men who are rich handle this in the wrong way. This is why our Lord said it is difficult for a rich man to enter into the kingdom of heaven.

The contrast our Lord draws between real, eternal riches and the present temporary shadows utterly contradicts the common view. We tend to regard spiritual things as shadowy, unreal things and earthly wealth as the real thing.

4. *In the other world we shall have what is our own.* In this life we are handling what belongs to Another. "If you have not been trustworthy with someone else's property, who will give you property of your own?" We have already seen that the clear Scripture teaching is that no man owns a thing. When we depart from this life, we leave all material possessions behind. But, in the next world, what we possess will be our own. The solemn truth is that the use we make of our possessions and opportunities in this life will determine what we will possess of our own in the other world. How poor some rich Christians will be over there!

5. *Faithfulness in very little here is the mark of faithfulness in very much over there.* "Whoever can be trusted with very little can

also be trusted with much, and whoever is dishonest with very little will also be dishonest with much." However great our possessions here may be, they amount to very little compared with the riches of that other world. We have already noted in the study of the parable of the minas that the man who earned twenty-five thousand dollars from his twenty-five hundred dollars was made ruler over ten cities.

This parable as well as that of the minas suggests the principle that the Lord is here testing His servants and training them for future responsibilities and opportunities that go far beyond anything we can imagine. As a store owner watches a young employee who is faithful in performing minor tasks and recognizes that he will be faithful in handling much more important matters, so our Lord sees a faithful Sunday school teacher or a faithful homemaker and recognizes that they are training to take care of great responsibilities in the unseen, spiritual world.

6. *Every person must choose between serving the present world and serving God:* "No servant can serve two masters. Either he will hate the one and love the other, or he will be devoted to the one and despise the other. You cannot serve both God and Money." This is an uncompromising statement. In actual life we find that Christians are seeking to do exactly this—holding on to the things of the world and at the same time not wanting to be cut off from God. Our Lord gives the truth in an absolute form so that we may be startled into recognizing that there is a clear line between God and the world.

In even stronger language the Spirit speaks through John:

> Do not love the world or anything in the world. If anyone loves the world, the love of the Father is not in him. For everything in the world—the cravings of sinful man, the lust of his eyes and the boasting of what he has and does— comes not from the Father but from the world. The world and its desires pass away, but the man who does the will of God lives forever. (1 John 2:15-17)

The challenge is to follow Christ as our Master and to hate everything that is contrary to His standards of life. It is possible for Christians to love some worldly thing, but when true Christians are walking after the flesh they are not comfortable in doing so. They will find their true life only in holding to their true Master and despising the world. When Christians are serving God with their whole heart and mind, they cannot love money, and when they are seeking the things of the world they are not serving their God and setting their hearts on Him.

7. *The parable appeals to us to lay up treasures in heaven.* "But store up for yourselves treasures in heaven, where moth and rust do not destroy, and where thieves do not break in and steal. For where your treasure is, there your heart will be also" (Matt. 6:20-21).

This laying up of treasure in heaven is represented in the parable by the manager making earthly friends who received him into their houses after he is dismissed. Our Lord's application is: "I tell you, use worldly wealth to gain friends for yourselves, so that when it is gone, you will be welcomed into eternal dwelings." As the manager enjoyed the comfort of being cared for by his friends because he provided for that very thing while he handled the money, so we Christians will have the treasures and riches of the eternal world if we are faithful in our present stewardship.

It has been asked what these "eternal dwellings" are and whether we are received into them by believers whom we have helped to win for Christ or by the angels. But it is not necessary for us to go into such details. In the story, the manager's foresight and prudence provided him with dwelling places. These earthly dwellings would naturally be set over against "the eternal dwellings," referring neither to specific dwellings nor to angels receiving us, but referring to all of the provisions in that other world that are made richer because of our investments here.

Paul sums up the attitude that he as a faithful steward had toward the suffering and trials of this present age. "So we fix our eyes not on what is seen, but on what is unseen. For what is seen is temporary, but what is unseen is eternal" (2 Cor. 4:18). This is one of those striking, direct teachings in the Epistles that carry out the message of our Lord's parables on stewardship.

The Personal Application

The Master's message on money is to use money to provide for the needs of ourselves and for those for whom we are responsible in this world, and to use *all the rest* for one purpose only—to be rich toward God, laying up treasure in heaven. It is not accurate to say that one tenth of our money belongs to God and nine tenths to ourselves.

It is certainly well for Christians to set aside a minimum of one tenth for the Lord's service as a recognition of God's ownership of the whole ten tenths. It may require all of the nine tenths to provide for our necessities. But in the case of those who have more money than they require for personal needs, they should see that it is wisely invested. And the only wise investment is in God's treasury.

Some teach that the tithe is something we pay to God, just as the Jews were required to pay their tithe and that only what is given in addition to the tenth is really given to God. But everything that we give as to the Lord is a gift, not a payment. For many who have little income, the payment of a tenth is indeed sacrificial giving, and every cent of it is given to the Lord as definitely and truly as the offerings of Christians who give far beyond the tenth.

The Jews gave more than one tenth, but it must be remembered that their giving was part of the legal system of the kingdom. It included what we would call taxes for the maintenance of civic affairs and government, as well as for the maintenance of worship services. Everything was, indeed, for the service of God, who was their King, and so the tithes and the free-will offerings were given to Him. The Christian should give systematically and regularly, and those who have adopted the tithe as a minimum have found great blessing in this practice.

This is not suggesting that Christians are under a legal obligation to give a tithe but that when they do give systematically, it should be done on a regular basis. Those able to give more should not confine their giving to a tenth.

The call of Christian stewardship is far higher than the call of law in the Old Testament. We are called to be "Macedonian givers." The members of the church in Macedonia gave out of their extreme poverty, with generosity. They gave beyond their power. They had caught the message of Christian stewardship (2 Cor. 8:1-7). The appeal for our giving is the grace of our Lord Jesus Christ, who "though he was rich, yet for your sakes he became poor, so that you through his poverty might become rich" (v. 9). God loves a cheerful giver, and His plea to us to sow bountifully is that we might also reap bountifully. Paul gives a great commentary on the parable of the shrewd manager in 2 Corinthians 9:6-15.

In his first letter Paul's instruction to the Corinthians concerning Christian giving follows immediately the great resurrection chapter, with its stirring closing exhortation. "Therefore, my dear brothers, stand firm. Let nothing move you. Always give yourselves fully to the work of the Lord, because you know that your labor in the Lord is not in vain" (1 Cor. 15:58). Then comes the statement, "Now about the collection for God's people" (16:1).

There is no apology here for speaking of money. There is no mention that we have gone from the glories of spiritual things to an unpleasant subject. The Christian use of money is also one of the high spiritual privileges in which we are to abound.

Paul then gives a method: "On the first day of every week, each one of you should set aside a sum of money in keeping with his income, saving it up, so that when I come no collections will have to be made" (v. 2).

This parable on stewardship has, we see, a very direct bearing on the Christian use of money. The Pharisees who heard the parable recognized this: "The Pharisees, who loved money, heard all this and were sneering at Jesus." They were "people of the world." In their case the love of money was a root of all kinds of evil (1 Tim. 6:10). Judas also was a lover of money; and he and the Pharisees joined to crucify Christ.

Our Lord gives the Pharisees a stern and solemn answer: "You are the ones who justify yourselves in the eyes of men, but God knows your hearts. What is highly valued among men is detestable in God's sight." The Scriptures recognize that men always applaud those who love money. The world applauds those who do well for themselves and looks askance at those who are "other-worldly," especially in their use of money. How startling and terrible is our Lord's statement that money and honor and pride, which are exalted among men, are detestable in the sight of God.

While the parable does have this direct application to money, we can realize that its teaching goes much deeper. It concerns the stewardship of life, time, gifts, and everything we handle here in this present world. We should handle it all in view of the fact that the unseen world is the real and eternal world, while this present world is but a preparation for the one that is to come.

It is right that we should put Christ into present living; it is right that we should enjoy the indwelling of the Spirit and make this life all it can be. It is also right that we should strive in every way to alleviate the sufferings of the poor and improve conditions in city, state, and nation. The greatest social accomplishments have been those that have followed in the wake of Christian missionaries preaching Christ.

But when all is said that should be said about this present life and its possibilities, we still need to remember that the true meaning and significance of this life is in relation to the eternity that is to follow. It is no accident that those who have cast off the truth of God's Word are those who find little or no meaning in the present life, in spite of their efforts to improve it. For this life has no true meaning apart from that unseen, spiritual world. Our part here is to lay up treasure in heaven, and we will then have promise of the life that now is, as well as that which is to come (1 Tim. 4:8).

Why Angels Are Surprised

> The angels from their thrones on high
> Look down on us with wondering eye,
> That where we are but passing guests
> We build such strong and solid nests,
> But where we hope to dwell for aye
> We scarce take heed one stone to lay.

REVIEW OF LESSON 14

1. What is the spiritual message in the friends' receiving the manager into their houses?

2. What is meant by the "eternal dwellings"?

3. What does this parable teach about the use of money?

4. What is the New Testament teaching concerning tithing and giving money?

5. What does this parable teach about the relationship between this world and the eternal world?

PREPARATION FOR LESSON 15

Reading Lesson: Luke 16:14-31

1. The parable of the shrewd manager was spoken especially to the disciples. For whom was the parable of the rich man and Lazarus intended, and why?

2. Why did the rich man go to torment and Lazarus to bliss?

3. Does this parable apply only to the rich neglecting the poor, or does its teaching go beyond this?

4. Do you think the rich man's words indicate a change of heart?

5. What was his motive in asking Abraham to send new light to his brothers?

Lesson 15

The Rich Man and Lazarus

Luke 16:19-31

With the story of the rich man and Lazarus we come to the parable that has caused more controversy than perhaps any other. First of all, there is the dispute as to whether this is a parable or the record of actual fact. Some earnest students even make it a test of loyalty to the Bible, suggesting that one who teaches this as a parable is weakening the authority of God's Word. But it should be clearly understood at the outset that the teaching is in no wise affected by the question of whether our Lord is using a historical event or simply using a parable to illustrate the truth.

One reason given for regarding the narrative as actual history is the opening statement: "There was a rich man." Some suppose that the Lord had a definite historical character in view. But the same type of introduction is used in the parables of the unmerciful servant (Matt. 18:23), the two sons (21:28), the tenants (v. 33), the wedding banquet (22:2), the rich fool (Luke 12:16), the great banquet (14:16), and the ten minas (19:12). It is evidently a common way for beginning a parable and so is an argument in favor of regarding this as a parable.

An argument more often advanced against regarding it as a

187

parable is that the name Lazarus is given to the poor man while no other parable gives a name to one of the characters. But in this parable it would have been most unnatural for Lazarus not to have a name, since the rich man refers to him by his name. In other parables, the necessities of the story do not require that the characters be named. Moreover, the name Lazarus means one who is helped by God, and this is an important point in the story for it indicates that the poor man was a true believer in God.

It is also argued that a parable is an earthly story, representing some spiritual truth, while in this narrative the spiritual truth is contained in the story, for it teaches that the wrong use of riches here will result in loss and punishment afterwards. But this story of the rich man and Lazarus is but one striking and extreme illustration of the great spiritual truth presented by the parable, namely, the relation of this present world, and our actions in it, to the unseen, eternal world.

While the great truths intended are not affected by this matter of actual occurrence or parable, yet there are conclusive reasons for treating it as a parable. If this were a record of actual fact, it would be reasonable to suppose that it happened during the earthly lifetime of our Lord. The five brothers of the rich man would be living and would be well known in the community. It is inconceivable that our Lord would use a story like this that would instantly turn attention to this family. It would be contrary to His practice and would be the only instance of such personal reference in His teaching.

Indeed, we may say that the Lord studiously avoided any personal references of this kind that would tend to divert attention from the great truth He was presenting. One of the primary reasons for teaching in parables was to set the truth out where it could be considered apart from personal prejudices and views. Again, the story of the rich man and Lazarus is preceded by six parables, and it forms a companion to the parable of the shrewd manager, pressing home the great message of stewardship from another viewpoint. There is every reason, therefore, for regarding it as a parable, as practically all the great commentators have done.

There is another more important reason why special interest attaches to this parable. Its references to the next life and to the condition of saved and lost people when they die are so definite that it has frequently been studied in connection with these doctrines rather than for its main message. There are those who regard its references to the other world as entirely figurative and as expressing Jewish views that Christ did not necessarily endorse. It is probably because of such teaching that certain teachers have insisted that the narrative is not a parable but actual history, supposing that this is the best answer to those who would discount Christ's teaching on life after death.

But we cannot suppose that the Lord would use erroneous ideas about the future life in a parable. We have seen that the parable stories are true to life; and if there is nothing in them contrary to the natural experience of men as we know it here on earth, surely our Lord would give nothing contrary to the facts of the unseen world.

This parable is an unanswerable argument against those who teach that death is annihilation or that it is a state of unconsciousness or soul sleep. One of the leading advocates of soul sleep, recognizing this clear teaching, considers this narrative as neither a record of fact nor a parable but as a sample of false Pharisaic teaching, given by Christ to illustrate how they made God's laws void by their tradition! The teachings concerning the future life will be considered when the message of the parable is studied. They are mentioned here so that we may realize the great importance of this parable.

The Setting (Luke 16:14-18)

The parable of the shrewd manager forms a real part of the setting of this second parable recorded in Luke 16. The same groups are before our Lord as those mentioned in connection with the parables of the lost sheep, the lost coin, and the lost son. There are the tax collectors and sinners who have come to the Lord, His own apostles and disciples, and the scribes and Pharisees murmuring against Him. We have seen that when He gave the parable of the shrewd manager, "the Pharisees, who loved money, heard all this and were sneering at Jesus."

Our Lord answered that though they justified themselves in the sight of men, God knew their hearts, and that "what is highly valued among men is detestable in God's sight." Then several statements about the law and divorce that are regarded by many interpreters as "detached saying," having no special connection with what goes before or follows. But the connection is a close and vital one, though the sayings are probably reported by Luke in an abbreviated form.

These Pharisees claimed to be teachers of the law. They were enemies of Christ, having rejected the testimony of John the Baptist and that of their Messiah. They were evidently guilty of the three great sins of the human heart: lust, greed, and pride. The parable of the lost son spoke to their spiritual pride and their hatred of tax collectors and sinners. The parable of the shrewd manager spoke to their greed, for they were lovers of money.

One of the terrible evils against which our Lord preached was divorce, and His teachings reveal the low morals of the day. With this background, we can understand that when our Lord spoke of the spiritual condition of the Pharisees He would refer to the Law and the Prophets and then would go on to speak to this matter of divorce (Luke 16:16-18).

These Pharisees gloried in the law; Christ reminded them

that the Law and the Prophets were until John, and that from the time of John the Baptist the good news of the kingdom of God was preached. They were rejecting this message, refusing to believe that the kingdom of God was at hand.

The expression "everyone is forcing his way into it" is a difficult one. The favored view is that men take it by violence, in a good sense, breaking with their old ideas. In this present passage our Lord is teaching that the gospel of the kingdom of God does not do away with the Law and the Prophets, but rather fulfills them. "Forcing his way into it" may mean that men misunderstood the kingdom and sought to bring about by force that which will come in a natural, orderly way, with its right relation to the Law and the Prophets that have gone before.

In any case, it is plain that the revelation of God the Pharisees had in the Law and the Prophets will judge them in the life to come, as is indicated in the parable. As an illustration of the truth that the law will not fall, our Lord gives its teaching on adultery. His own teaching, in the kingdom of God, reveals the true inner meaning of God's law in this matter and raises the standard in such a way that the Pharisees are condemned for the way they dealt with sexual matters, just as they are condemned for their wrong use of money. Then follows the story of the rich man and Lazarus, which is evidently directed against the Pharisees and is a warning to them.

It is said that some, or many, of the Pharisees lived moderate lives; but there were others among them who lived luxuriously. However, it is not merely their use of material things that is in question but also their handling of all of the "deposit" that had been committed to them, including their spiritual leadership, which they were prostituting by not showing mercy to the tax collectors and sinners who were seeking salvation.

The Story (Luke 16:19-31)

Nearly all the characteristics of the parable stories seem to be combined in this unforgettable picture of the rich man and Lazarus. Full of human interest, vivid, startling, intense action, every sentence pregnant with meaning, it would be difficult to crowd more into such brief passage.

The rich man, clothed in the purple and fine linen that are the marks of the greatest luxury in clothing, lived in luxury every day. He is not held up as a dishonest man, nor as a drunkard. There is nothing sinful in purple and fine linen, nor is there necessarily anything sinful in feasting. The evil is in what lies back of a life that is given to feasting every day.

The "beggar named Lazarus" affords the opportunity to see the rich man's life in its true light. The story presents the extremes of luxury and need. In a most striking way the two men are brought together. Lazarus is laid at the rich man's gate, where the rich man sees him daily as he enters his mansion. Lazarus is full of sores. The dogs are probably more an indication of his extreme need rather than a sign of some comfort being extended to him in the absence of human sympathy. Given the opportunity, Lazarus would have eaten the crumbs that fell from the rich man's table. But the rich man ignored the beggar; so he didn't even get crumbs.

When the beggar died, he was carried away by the angels to "Abraham's side." The Jews used this expression as a figure for the blessed abode of departed spirits. Abraham was the father of all who have faith, and his side refers to the place of salvation and blessing. Today, now that Christ has died and risen again, believers depart and go to be with Christ. The rich man also died and was buried. Doubtless he had a magnificent funeral, but nothing is said of the angels carrying him to Abraham's side. Angels are ministering spirits, sent to serve those who are the heirs of salvation (Heb. 1:14).

The picture of the rich man in hell, seeing Abraham far off and Lazarus by his side and conversing with Abraham is not to be taken literally. However, the truth expressed in this story is very real. In hell the rich man was in torment. When he cried out to Abraham, we are not to suppose there was actually a flame and that he would be relieved by water applied to his tongue. This is a figure for real torment, and it is a vivid picture of the reversal of the earthly condition of the two men. The rich man now cries to Lazarus for mercy, to whom he had shown no mercy.

Abraham reminds him that in his lifetime he had received good things and Lazarus evil things. This does not mean that the rich man was in torment because he received good things on earth, nor that Lazarus was in bliss because he received evil things on earth. But it does remind the rich man that he had lived for the riches and pleasures of earthly life. How vivid are those words: "Son, remember." But apart from this, Abraham says, his request cannot possibly be fulfilled because of the great gulf fixed between him and Lazarus.

The rich man then requests that Abraham send to his father's house and warn his five brothers. They evidently were living the same kind of life he had lived. This request appears to indicate that the rich man's heart was softened and that he desired to save his brothers. However, we must note that he was not concerned about the evil lives of his brothers but "that they will not also come to this place of torment." It is evident that his concern was not primarily with his brothers. The rich man is suggesting that he had not had suitable warning.

Abraham answers that they have Moses and the prophets.

The rich man asks once again, and this shows that he believed he did not have proper warning on earth concerning the place of torment.

Abraham answered, "If they do not listen to Moses and the Prophets, they will not be convinced even if someone rises from the dead."

The Spiritual Message

The central message of this parable is one of stewardship. It is a fearful picture of a man who was unfaithful as a steward on earth and who reaped torment in the unseen, spiritual world. It is an appeal to Christians to use their wealth as an opportunity to lay up treasure in heaven. This parable is a warning against unfaithfulness, directed especially to the Pharisees. It is a message to those who sin against light, who have God's Word concerning the real meanings of life. This parable also lifts the veil between the present material world and the unseen eternal world, revealing that the way we handle our stewardship here will decide what the other life will be.

Along with this central message of stewardship, there are tremendous facts concerning the other life given in the parable. Some teach that it is a mistake to draw doctrine from parables. But parables are given to teach, and when correctly interpreted they give us true doctrine. We must draw no teaching from a parable that is contrary to anything else revealed in the Word, but in this parable the truths concerning the unseen world confirm the revelation in the rest of Scripture and are just as authoritative as direct teaching would be. Let us note these truths and then consider how they relate to the central message.

1. *At death there is continued consciousness.* The separation of the spirit from the body does not mean that the spirit is annihilated or that it goes into a state of unconsciousness. There are those who teach that the soul sleeps until the resurrection day, when it is reunited with the body. This teaching is associated with the view that there is no distinction between soul and body. But everything that Scripture says concerning man takes for granted that man is a living soul, dwelling in a body, and that when we die we simply put off this body (2 Peter 1:14).

Christians depart and go to be with Christ (Phil. 1:23). The Bible also takes for granted the fact that man's spirit continues its existence without end. There is no suggestion of "conditional immortality." We are told that "the mortal" will put on "immortality." That is, the body, the part of man that is subject to death, will put on immortality; "the perishable," that is, the part that is subject to decay, will be clothed "with the imperishable" (1 Cor. 15:53).

2. *The lost go into conscious torment, the saved into conscious bliss.* It is important to remember that lost people are tormented, not tortured. Nowhere is God represented as arbitrarily torturing men as punishment for sin. But in this parable, as elsewhere, the lost man reaps what he has sown and is in "torment" because this is what he laid up for himself when on earth.

Lazarus is in the place of comfort, represented figuratively as "Abraham's side." Abraham, Isaac, and Jacob are now living and are in the blessedness of God's presence. God is the God of the living (Matt. 22:32). Moses and Elijah were very much alive and were very keenly interested in the work of the Lord Jesus when they appeared before Him during the Transfiguration. They are alive and conscious at this moment, and what is true of them is true of all who have died in Christ.

This condition of conscious torment and conscious bliss immediately following death should be distinguished from the eternal state. The saved who are with Christ look forward to the day when they and we will have our resurrection bodies and redemption will be complete. Lost people await the day of the judgment of the Great White Throne, when their bodies also will be raised and when the lost will be cast into the lake of fire that is "the second death" (Rev. 20:14).

3. *There is a great gulf fixed between the saved and lost, and this condition is unchangeable.* This solemn truth clearly indicates that our destiny is fixed by our choices in this life, and there is no

chance to reverse this choice after death. Our Lord would not have used these words in the parable unless they taught this truth.

4. *Earthly choices determine eternal destiny, and earthly inequalities are adjusted in the next life.* There is no explanation of the sufferings of the righteous except in relation to that unseen, eternal world. Lazarus believed in God, and God in His love permitted him to suffer, even as He permitted Job to suffer. Job had a foretaste of God's abounding grace while still on earth. In the case of Lazarus, there was no compensation on earth. But the same principles set forth in Job apply to Lazarus. His "troubles," which were for the moment, worked out for him "an eternal glory" (2 Cor. 4:17).

The rich man in this parable was a son of this present age and lived as though there were no life beyond this. He was not rich toward God. Human reason tells us that a man who lives wholly for the things of the flesh will be in torment when he does not have the flesh nor the means of satisfying the flesh.

5. *God has given ample light and ample warning to every man on earth to seek eternal things.* The application is certainly to the Jew, who had the light of revelation in the Old Testament. The rich man's request that Abraham send Lazarus to warn his five brothers was a complaint against God that He did not make plain the reality of the unseen world. Paul makes clear in Romans that the heathen, who do not have the written revelation, nevertheless are without excuse, because God has given them the light of nature, and they are sinning against this light in not seeking God (Rom. 1:20-21).

These Pharisees to whom our Lord was speaking were rejecting the voice of God coming to them through the Messiah, the One who came directly from that unseen world. Moreover, when the Lord Jesus died and rose again, most of them still rejected Him. How solemn is the prophecy given in the parable as the word of Abraham: "If they do not listen to Moses and the Prophets, they will not be convinced even if someone rises from the dead." A real Lazarus did rise from the dead, an event that was a type of the great resurrection of our Lord. For nineteen hundred years, Christ's death and resurrection have been proclaimed, but men have turned a deaf ear, even as the Pharisees did to the message given through Moses and the prophets.

It may be argued that one so heartless and callous to human needs as this rich man would be the exception or that many men who reject Christ as their Savior seem to have real concern for the needs of others and are liberal in their philanthropy. But the picture given in the parable, which is purposely an extreme one, is a true picture of men who live with self at the center, whether expressed just as the rich man expressed it or not. These are men who live for what is exalted among men but is an abomination in the sight of God. Our Lord said to these Pharisees, "How can you believe if you accept praise from one another, yet make no effort to obtain the praise that comes from the only God?" (John 5:44).

Wealth and riches are the symbol of the glory of man. We often measure others and institutions by the yardstick of wealth. Nations, seeking to excel over one another, make money their god. This race for wealth has precipitated many wars. All this is an abomination in the sight of God, and our Lord's most fearful warnings are directed against the love of money, which stands for the love of the things of this world and a lack of belief in the reality of the eternal world.

The parable, therefore, presses home the same central message as the parable of the shrewd manager, except that this is a warning concerning the fearful results for those who do not make "friends" for themselves through the just use of worldly wealth (Luke 16:9). The rich man attempted in vain to get some temporary relief from Lazarus, the one to whom he gave no relief on earth.

All the parables of stewardship send out their clarion call: Lay up for yourselves treasures in heaven. Be rich toward God. Do all that you do here in view of the unseen, eternal world.

REVIEW OF LESSON 15

1. In your opinion, is this a parable or actual history?

2. How does this parable affect the teaching that death means annihilation? That death means unconsciousness until the resurrection? That there is a second chance after death? That all men are saved?

3. Do you think this parable applied to Pharisees who were not living in luxury? How does it apply to rich and poor today?

4. What does this parable teach us about the importance of the Word of God?

5. How does the central message of this parable differ from the central message of the parable of the shrewd manager?

APPENDIXES

1

PARABLES IN THE BIBLE

	Matthew	Mark	Luke
The Sower (The Four Kinds of Soil)	13	4	8
The Mustard Seed	13	4	13
The Tenants	21	12	20
The Yeast	13		13
The Lost Sheep	18		15
The Waiting Servant	24		12
The Weeds	13		
The Hidden Treasure	13		
The Pearl of Great Value	13		
The Net	13		
The Unmerciful Servant	18		
The Workers in the Vineyard	20		
The Two Sons	21		
The Wedding Banquet	22		
The Ten Virgins	25		
The Talents	25		
The Growing Seed		4	
The Watching Servant		13	
The Two Debtors			7
The Good Samaritan			10
The Friend at Midnight			11
The Rich Fool			12
Servants Awaiting Absent Master			12
The Barren Fig Tree			13
The Lowest Seat at the Feast			14
The Great Banquet			14
The Lost Coin			15
The Lost Son			15
The Shrewd Manager			16
The Rich Man and Lazarus			16
The Unworthy Servant			17
The Persistent Widow			18
The Pharisee and the Tax Collector			18
The Ten Minas			19
The Sheep Pen (usually classed as an allegory)		John 10:1-6	

2

PARABLE-SIMILES IN THE BIBLE

	Matthew	*Mark*	*Luke*
Salt without saltiness	5:13	9:50	14:34-35
Lamp under a bowl	5:15	4:21	8:16
Guests of the bridegroom	9:15	2:19-20	5:34-35
Unshrunk cloth on old garments	9:16	2:21	5:36
New wine in old wineskins	9:17	2:22	5:37-39
Kingdom and household divided	12:25	3:24-25	11:17
Tying a strong man	12:29	3:27	11:21-22
Yeast of Pharisees and Sadducees	16:6	8:15	12:1
Fig tree's leaves	24:32	13:28	21:29-31
Removing the eye and the hand	5:29-30	9:43-48	
Uncleanness is within	15:18	7:15	
Children's bread tossed to dogs	15:26	7:27	
Settling disputes quickly	5:25		12:58
Storing treasure in heaven	6:19-21		12:33-34
Eye: the lamp of the body	6:22		11:34
The birds (ravens)	6:26		12:24
The lilies	6:28		12:27
The speck and the plank	7:3-5		6:41-42
Good gifts to children	7:9-12		11:11-13
Tree known by its fruit	7:17-20		6:43-45
Wise and foolish builders	7:24-27		6:46-49
Reed swayed by wind	11:7-8		7:24-25
Children in the marketplace	11:16-17		7:31-32
Animal in the pit	12:11-12		14:5
Return of an evil spirit	12:43-45		11:24-26
Blind leading the blind	15:14		6:39
Cleaning the outside of a cup	23:25-26		11:39-40
Watching for thief	24:42-44		12:39
Giving in secret	6:2-4		
Houseowner's storeroom	13:52		
Plants uprooted	15:13		
Kings of earth and taxes	17:25-27		
Sheep and goats	25:31-33		
The narrow door			13:22-30
Building a tower			14:28-29
King going to war			14:31-33
Selling a cloak, buying a sword			22:36

3

PARABOLIC SAYINGS
IN THE SYNOPTIC GOSPELS

	Matthew	*Mark*	*Luke*
"With the measure you use, it will be measured to you."	7:2	4:24	6:38
"It is not the healthy who need a doctor, but the sick."	9:12	2:17	5:31
"Only in his home town and in his own house is a prophet without honor."	13:57	6:4	4:24
"No one can serve two masters."	6:24		16:13
"Foxes have holes and birds of the air have nests, but the Son of Man has no place to lay his head."	8:20		9:58
"Follow me, and let the dead bury their own dead."	8:22		9:60
"The harvest is plentiful but the workers are few."	9:37		10:2
"A student is not above his teacher, nor a servant above his master."	10:24		6:40
"A city on a hill cannot be hidden."	5:14		
"Physician, heal yourself!"			4:23
"No one who puts his hand to the plow and looks back is fit for service in the kingdom of God."			9:62
"For who is greater, the one who is at the table or the one who serves? Is it not the one who is at the table? But I am among you as one who serves."			22:27

4

PARABOLIC SAYINGS IN JOHN'S GOSPEL

"The wind blows wherever it pleases." (3:8)

"The friend who attends the bridegroom waits and listens for him, and is full of joy when he hears the bridegroom's voice. That joy is mine, and it is now complete." (3:29—the words of John the Baptist)

"Open your eyes and look at the fields! They are ripe for harvest." (4:35)

"A slave has no permanent place in the family, but a son belongs to it forever." (8:35)

"As long as it is day, we must do the work of him who sent me. Night is coming, when no one can work." (9:4)

"Are there not twelve hours of daylight? A man who walks by day will not stumble, for he sees by this world's light. It is when he walks by night that he stumbles, for he has no light." (11:9-10)

"Unless a kernel of wheat falls to the ground and dies, it remains only a single seed. But if it dies, it produces many seeds." (12:24)

"A person who has had a bath needs only to wash his feet; his whole body is clean." (13:10)

"No servant is greater than his master, nor a messenger greater than the one who sent him." (13:16; 15:20)

"A woman giving birth to a child has pain because her time has come; but when her baby is born she forgets the anguish because of her joy that a child is born into the world." (16:21)